The Poetry of Robert Greene

Robert Greene was, by the best accounts available, born in Norwich in 1558 and baptised on July 11th.

Greene is believed to have been a pupil at Norwich Grammar School and then attended Cambridge receiving his B.A. in 1580, and an M.A. in 1583. He then moved to London and began an extraordinary chapter in his life as a widely published author.

His literary career began with the publication of the long romance, 'Mamillia', (1580). Greene's romances were written in a highly wrought style which reached its peak in 'Pandosto' (1588) and 'Menaphon' (1589). Short poems and songs incorporated in some of the romances attest to his ability as a lyric poet.

In 1588, he was granted an MA from Oxford University, almost certainly as a courtesy degree. Thereafter he sometimes placed the phrase Utruisq. Academiae in Artibus Magister', "Master of Arts in both Universities" on the title page of his works.

The lack of records hinders any complete biography of Greene but he did write an autobiography of sorts, but where the balance lies between facts and artistic licence is not clearly drawn. According to that autobiography 'The Repentance of Robert Greene', Greene is alleged to have written 'A Groatsworth of Wit Bought with a Million of Repentance' during the month prior to his death, including in it a letter to his wife asking her to forgive him and stating that he was sending their son back to her.

His output was prolific. Between 1583 and 1592, he published more than twenty-five works in prose, becoming one of the first authors in England to support himself with his pen in an era when professional authorship was virtually unknown.

In his 'coney-catching' pamphlets, Greene fashioned himself into a well-known public figure, narrating colourful inside stories of rakes and rascals duping young gentlemen and solid citizens out of their hard-earned money. These stories, told from the perspective of a repentant former rascal, have been considered autobiographical, and to incorporate many facts of Greene's own life thinly veiled as fiction. However, the alternate account suggests that Greene invented almost everything, merely displaying his undoubted skills as a writer.

In addition to his prose works, Greene also wrote several plays, none of them published in his lifetime, including 'The Scottish History of James IV', 'Alphonsus', and his greatest popular success, 'Friar Bacon and Friar Bungay', as well as 'Orlando Furioso', based on Ludovico Ariosto's Orlando Furioso.

His plays earned himself the title as one of the 'University Wits', a group that included George Peele, Thomas Nashe, and Christopher Marlowe.

Robert Greene died 3rd September 1592.

Index of Contents

INTRODUCTION TO A MAIDENS DREAME

This poem had long disappeared, and was not known to be in existence till 1845, when it was discovered by Mr. James P. Reardon, who sent a transcript of it to the Council of the Shakespeare Society, among whose papers it was printed. Dyce incorporated it in the second edition of his Greene, but neither Mr. Reardon's transcript nor Dyce's is quite accurate. The original, a quarto of ten leaves—4to in Roman letter— is now in the library of Lambeth Palace. It has been transcribed for my text, and is here exactly reproduced.

A MAIDENS DREAME

Vpon the Death of the right Honorable Sir Christopher Hatton Knight, late Lord Chancelor of England

To the right worshipful, bountifull and vertuous Ladie, the Ladie Elizabeth Hatton, wife to the right Worshipful Sir William Hatton Knight, increase of all honorable vertues.

THE EPISTLE DEDICATORIE

Mourning as well as many (right Worshipfull Ladie) for the late losse of the right Honorable your deceased Unckle, whose death being the common preiudice of the present age, was lamented of most (if not all) and I among the rest sorrowing that my Countrie was depriued of him that liued not for himselfe, but for his Countrie, I began to call to mind what a subiect was ministred to the excellent wits of both Vniuersities to work vpon, when so worthie a Knight, and so vertuous a Iusticiarie, had by his death left many memorable actions performed in his life, deseruing highly by some rare pen to be registred. Passing ouer many daies in this muse, at last I perceiued mens humors slept, that loue of many friends followed no farther then their graues, that Art was growen idle, and either choice schollers feared to write of so high a subiect as his vertues, or else they dated their deuotions no farther then his life. While thus I debated with my selfe, I might see (to the great disgrace of the Poets of our time) some Mycanicall wits blow vp Mountaines, and bring forth mise, who with their follies did rather disparage his Honors, than decypher his vertues: beside, as Virtutis comes est inuidia, so base report who hath her tong blistered by slanderous enuie, began as farre as she durst, now after his death, to murmure, who in his life time durst not once mutter: wherupon touched with a zealous jealousie ouer his wonderfull vertues, I could not, whatsoeuer discredit I reapt by my presumption, although I did Tenui Auena meditari, but discouer the honorable qualities of so worthie a Counsellor, nor for anie priuat benefit I euer had of him, which should induce me fauorably to flatter his worthie partes, but onely that I shame to let slip with silence, the vertues and honors of so worthie a Knight, whose deserts had bin so many and so great towards al. Therfore (right worshipful Ladie) I drewe a fiction called A Maidens Dreame, which as it is Enigmatically so it is not without some speciall and considerate reasons.—Whose slender

Muse I present vnto your Ladiship, induced therunto, first, that I know you are partaker of your husbands sorrowes for the death of his honourable Uncle, and desire to heare his honors put in memorie after his death, as you wished his aduancement in vertues to be great in his life: as also that I am your Ladishippes poore Countriman, and haue long time desired to gratifie your right worshipfull father with some thing worthie him selfe. Which because I could not to my Content performe, I haue now taken oportunitie to shew my duetie to him in his daughter, although the gift be farre too meane for so worshipfull and vertuous a Lady. Yet hoping your Ladishippe will with courtesie fauour my presuming follies, and in gratious acceptance vouch of my well meant labours,

I humbly take my leaue.

Your Ladiships humbly at Commaund
R. Greene. Nordovicensis.

A MAIDENS DREAME

Methovght in slumber as I lay and dreamt,
I sawe a silent spring raild in with leat,
From sunnie shade or murmur quite exempt
The glide whereof gainst weeping flints did beat,
And round about were leauelesse beeches set,
So darke, it seemed nights mantle for to borrow,
And well to be the gloomie den of sorrow.

About this spring in mourning roabes of blacke,
Were sundrie Nymphs or Goddesses, me thought,
That seemly sate in rankes iust backe to backe,
On Mossie benches Nature there had wrought.
And cause the wind and spring no murmure brought
They fild the aire with such laments and groanes,
That Eccho sigh'd out their heart-breaking mones.

Elbow on knee, and head vpon their hand,
As mourners sit, so sat these Ladies all,
Garlands of Eben-bowes whereon did stand,
A golden crowne, their mantles were of pall,
And from their waterie eies warme teares did fall,
With wringing hands they sat and sigh'd like those,
That had more griefe then well they could disclose.

I lookt about and by the fount I spied,
A Knight lie dead, yet all in armour clad,
Booted and spurd, a faulchion by his side,
A Crowne of Oliues on his helme he had,
As if in peace and war he were adrad,
A golden Hind was placed at his feet,

Whose valed eares bewraid her inward greet.

She seemed wounded by her panting breath,
Her beating breast with sighs did fall and rise,
Wounds was there none, it was her masters death,
That drew Electrum from her weeping eies,
Like scalding smoake her braying throbs outflies,
As Deere do mourne when arrow hath them galled
So was this Hinde with Hart-sicke pains inthralled.

Just at his head there sate a Sumptuous Queene,
I gest her so, for why she wore a crowne,
Yet were her garments parted white and greene,
Tierd like vnto the picture of renowne,
Vpon her lap she laid his head a downe,
Vnlike to all she smiled on his face,
Which made me long to know this dead mans case.

As thus I lookt, gan Iustice to arise,
I knew the Goddes by her equall beame,
And dewing on his face balme from her eies,
She wet his visage with a yearnfuli streame,
Sad mournfull lookes did from her arches gleame,
And like to one, whom sorrow deep attaints,
With heaued hands she poureth forth these plaints.

THE COMPLAINT OF JVSTICE

Vntoward Twins that tempers humane fate,
Who from your distaffe draws the life of man
Pane impartiall to the highest state,
Too soone you cut what Clotho earst began,
Your fatall doomes this present age may ban,
For you have robd the world of such a Knight,
As best coyuld skil to ballance Iustice right.

His eyes were seates for mercy and for law,
Fauour in one, and Iustice in the other:
The poore he smoth'd, the proud he kept in aw,
As iust to strangers as vnto his brother.
Bribes could not make him any wrong to smother,
For to a Lord, or to the lowest Groome:
Stil conscience and the cawes set down the doome.

Delaying law that picks the clients purse
Ne could this knight abide to heare debated

From day to day (that claimes the poor mans curse)
Nor might the pleas be ouer-long dilated.
Much shifts of law there was by him abated.
With conscience carefully he heard the cause:
Then gaue his doome with short dispatch of lawes.

The poore mans crie he thought a holy knell,
No sooner gan their suites to pearce his eares,
But faire-eyed pitie in his heart did dwell.
And like a father that affection beares
So tendred he the poore with inward teares.
And did redresse their wrongs when they did call:
But poore or rich he still was iust to all.

Oh wo is me (saith Iustice) he is dead,
The knight is dead that was so iust a man:
And in Astraeas lap low lies his head,
Who whilom wonders in the world did scan.
Iustice hath lost her chiefest lim, what than.
At this her sighes and sorowes were so sore:
And so she wept that she could speak no more.

THE COMPLAINT OF PRVDENCE

A wreath of Serpents bout her lilly wrist,
Did seemly Prudence weare: she then arose,
A siluer Doue satt mourning on her fist,
Teares on hir cheeks like dew vpon a rose,
And thus began the Goddesse greeful glose.
Let England mourn, for why? his daies are don
Whom Prudence nurced like her dearest sonne.

Hatton, at that I started in my dreame,
But not awooke: Hatton is dead quoth she,
Oh, could I pour out teares like to a streame,
A sea of them would not sufficient be,
For why our age had few more wise then he.
Like oracles, as were Apollos sawes:
So were his words accordant to the lawes.

Wisdome sate watching in his w r ary eyes,
His insight subtil, if vnto a foe, roo
He could with counsels Commonwelths comprise,
No forraine wit could Hattons ouergoe
Yet to a frend, wise, simple, and no mo.
His ciuill policie vnto the state

Scarce left behind him now a second mate.

For Countries weale his councel did exceede,
And Eagle-eyed he was to spie a fault:
For warres or peace right wisely could he reed:
Twas hard for trechors fore his lookes to hault.
The smooth-fac'd traitor could not him assault, no
As by his Countries loue his grees did rise,
So to his Countrey was he simple wise.

This graue aduiser of the Commonweale,
This prudent Counceller vnto his Prince,
Whose wit was busied with his Mistres heale,
Secret conspiracies could wel conuince,
Whose insight perced the sharp-eyed Linx.
He is dead, at this her sorowes were so sore:
And so she wept that she could speake no more.

THE COMPLAINT OF FORTITVDE

Next Fortitude arose vnto this Knight,
And by his side sate doun with stedfast eyes.
A broken Columb twixt her arms was pight
She could not weep nor pour out yernful cries,
From Fortitude sucn base affects nil rise.
Brass-renting Goddesse, she cannot lament,
Yet thus her plaints with breathing sighs were spent.

Within the Maidens Court, place of all places,
I did aduance a man of high desert:
Whom Nature had made proud with all her graces
Inserting courage in his noble heart,
No perils drad could euer make him start.
But like to Scaeuola, for countries good,
He did not value for to spend his blood.

His lookes were sterne, though in a life of peace.
Though not in warres, yet war hung in his browes:
His honor did by martiall thoughts increase,
To martiall men liuing this Knight allowes,
And by his sword he solemnly auowes
Thogh not in war, yet if that war were here,
As warriors do to value honor deere.

Captens he kept and fostered them with fee,
Soldiers were seruants to this martiall Knight,

Men might his stable full of coursers see,
Trotters, whose manag'd lookes would som afright.
His armorie was rich and warlike dight.
And he himselfe if any need had craued,
Would as stout Hector haue himselfe behaued.

I lost a frend when as I lost his life,
Thus playned Fortitude, and frownd withall,
Cursed be Atrapos, and curst her knife,
That made the Capten of my gard to fall,
Whose vertues did his honors high install.
At this she storm'd, and wrong out sighes so sore:
That what for grief her tongue could speak no more.

THE COMPLAINT OF TEMPERANCE

Then Temperance with bridle in her hand,
Did mildly look vpon this liuelesse Lord,
And like to weeping Niobe did stand,
Her sorrowes and her teares did wel accord,
Their Diapason was in selfe-same cord,
Here lies the man (quoth she) that breath'd out this:
To shun fond pleasures is the sweetest blisse.

No choice delight could draw his eyes awry,
He was not bent to pleasures fond conceits,
Inueigling pride, nor worlds sweet vanitie,
Loues luring follies with their strange deceits,
Could wrap this Lord within their baleful sleights.
But he despising all, said man was grasse:
His date a span, et omnia vanitas.

Temperate he was, and tempered al his deedes,
He brideled those affects that might offend,
He gaue his wil no more the raines then needs,
He measured pleasures euer by the end:
His thoughts on vertues censures did depend.
What booteth pleasures that so quickly passe,
When such delights are brickie like to glasse.

First pride of life, that subtil branch of sinne,
And then the lusting humor of the eyes
And base concupiscence which plies her gin,
These Sirens that doe worldlings stil intise,
Could not allure his mind to think of vice.
For he said stil, pleasures delight it is:

That holdeth man from heauens deliteful blisse.

Temperat he was in euery deep extreame,
And could wel bridle his affects with reason:
What I haue lost in loosing him then deeme
Base death, that tooke away a man so geason,
That measur'd euery thought by tyme and season.
At this her sighes and sorowes were so sore:
And so she wept that she could speake no more.

THE COMPLAINT OF BOVNTIE

With open hands, and mourning lockes dependant,
Bounty stept foorth to waile the dead mans losse.
On her was loue and plenty both attendant,
Teares in her eyes, armes folded quite acrosse:
Sitting by him vpon a turfe of mosse,
She sigh'd and said, here lies the knight deceased,
Whose bountie, Bounties glorie much increased.

His lookes were liberall, and in his face
Sate frank Magnificence with armes displaid:
His open hands discourst his inward grace:
The poore were neuer at their need denaid:
His careles scorn of gold his deedes bewraid.
And this he crau'd, no longer for to liue:
Then he had power, and mind, and wil to giue.

No man went emptie from his frank dispose,
He was a purse-bearer vnto the poore:
He wel obseru'd the meaning of this glose,
None lose reward that geueth of their store:
To all his bounty past. Ay me therefore
That he should die, with that she sigh'd so sore:
And so she wept that she could speak no more.

THE COMPLAINT OF HOSPITALITIE

Lame of a leg, as she had lost a lim
Start vp kind Hospitalitie and wept,
She silent sate awhile and sigh'd by him
As one halfe maymed to this knight she crept,
At last about his neck this Nimph she lept,
And with her Cornucopia in her fist,

For very loue his chilly lips she kist.

Ay me, quoth she, my loue is lorn by death,
My chiefest stay is crack t, and I am lame:
He that his almes franckly did bequeath,
And fed the poore with store of food: the same
Euen he is dead, and vanisht is his name.
Whose gates were open, and whose almes deede
Supplied the fatherlesse and widowes need.

He kept no Christmas house for once a yeere,
Each day his boards were fild with Lordly fare:
He fed a rout of yeomen with his cheare,
Nor was his bread and beefe kept in with care,
His wine and beere to strangers were not spare.
And yet beside to al that hunger greeued,
His gates were ope, and they were there releeued.

Wel could the poore tel where to fetch their bread,
As Bausis and Philemon were i blest
For feasting Iupiter in strangers stead,
So happy be his high immortal rest,
That was to hospitalitie addrest:
For few such Hue, and then she sigh'd so sore,
And so she wept that she could speak no more.

Then Courtesie whose face was full of smiles,
And frendship with her hand vpon her hart,
And tender Charitie that loues no wiles,
And Clemencie ther passions did impart.
A thousand vertues there did straight vp start,
And with ther teares and sighes they did disclose:
For Hattons death their harts were ful of woes.

THE COMPLAINT OF RELIGION

Next from the farthest nooke of all the place,
Weping full sore, there rose a nimph in black
Seemelie and sober with an Angels face,
And sighd as if her heart strings straight should crak
Hir outward woes bewraid her inward wracke.
A golden booke she caried in her hand,
It was religion that thus meeke did stand.

God wot her garments were full looslie tucked
As one that carelesse was in some despaire,

To tatters were her roabes and vestures pluckt
Her naked lims were open to the aire,
Yet for all this her lookes were blith and faire,
And wondring how religion grew forlorne,
I spied her roabes by Heresie was tome.

This holy creature sate her by this knight,
And sigh'd out this, oh here he lies (quoth she)
Liuelesse, that did religions lampe still light,
Deuout without dissembling, meeke and free
To such whose words and liuings did agree,
Lip-holines in Cleargie men he could not brooke,
Ne such as counted gold aboue their booke.

Vpright he liu'd, as holy writ him lead,
His faith was not in ceremonies old,
Nor had he new found toies within his head,
Ne was he luke-warme, neither hot nor colde,
But in religion he was constant bold,
And still a sworne professed fo to all,
Whose lookes were smooth, harts pharesaicall.

The brainsicke and illiterate surmisers,
That like to saints would holy be in lookes,
Of fond religions fabulous deuisers
Who scornd the Academies and their bookes,
And yet could sin as others in close nookes.
To such wild-headed mates he was a foe:
That rent her robes, and wronged Religion so.

Ne was his faith in mens traditions;
He hated Antichrist and all his trash:
He was not led away with superstitions,
Nor was he in religion ouer rash:
His hands from heresie he loued to wash.
Then base report, ware what thy tongue doth spred,
Tis sin and shame for to bely the dead.

Hart-holy men he still kept at his table,
Doctors that wel could doom of holie writ,
By them he knew to seuer faith from fable,
And how the text with iudgement for to hit:
For Pharisies in Moses chaire did sit.
At this Religion sigh'd and green* so sore:
And so she wept that she could speak no more.

PRIMATE(S)
Next might I see a rowt of Noble-men,

Earles, Barons, Lords, in mourning weedes attir'd:
I cannot paint their passions with my pen,
Nor write so queintly as their woes requir'd.
Their teares and sighs some Homers quil desir'd.
But this I know their grief was for his death:
That there had yeelded nature, life and breath:

MILITES
Then came by Souldiers trailing of their pikes,
Like men dismaid their beuers were adown;
Their warlike hearts his death with sorrow strikes;
Yea war him selfe was in a sable gowne:
For griefe you might perceiue his visage frowne:
And Scholers came by, with lamenting cries,
Wetting their bookes with teares fel from their eies.

PLEBS.
The common people they did throng in flocks,
Dewing their bosomes with their yernfull teares,
Their sighs were such as would haue rent the rocks,
Their faces ful of griefe, dismay and feares,
Their cries stroke pittie in my listning eares.
For why? the groanes are lesse at hels black gate,
Then Eccho there did then reuerberate.

Some came with scrolles and papers in their hand,
I ghest them sutors that did rue his losse:
Some with their children in their hand did stand,
Some poore and hungrie with their hands acrosse:
A thousand there sate wayling on the mosse.
O pater Patriae stil they cried thus:
Hatton is dead, what shal become of vs?

At all these cries my heart was sore amoued,
Which made me long to see the dead mans face:
What he should be that was so deare beloued,
Whose worth so deepe had won the peoples grace.
As I came pressing neere vnto the place,
I lookt, and though his face were pale and wan,
Yet by his visage I did know the man.

No sooner did I cast mine eie on him
But in his face there flasht a ruddie hue;
And though before his lookes by death were grim,
Yet seemd he smiling to my gazing view
(As if though dead, my presence still he knew:)
Seeing this change within a dead man's face,
I could not stop my teares, but wept a pace.

I cald to minde how that it was a knight,
That whilome liu'd in Englands happie soile,
I thought vpon his care and deepe insight,
For countries weale, his labour and his toile
He tooke, least that the English State might foile,
And how his watchfull thought from first had been
Vowed to the honor of the maiden Queene.

I cald to minde againe he was my friend,
And held my quiet as his hearts content;
What was so deare, for me he would not spend,
Then thoght I straight, such friends are seldom hent:
Thus still from loue to loue my humor went,
That pondering of his loyaltie so free,
I wept him dead, that liuing honord me.

At this Astraea seeing me so sad,
Gan blithly comfort me with this replie:
Virgin (quoth she) no boote by teares is had,
Nor doth laments ought pleasure them that die,
Soules must haue change from this mortalitie,
For liuing long sinne hath the larger space,
And dying well they finde the greater grace.

And sith thy teares bewraies thy loue (quoth she)
His soule with me shall wend vnto the skies,
His liuelesse bodie I will leaue to thee,
Let that be earthde and tombde in gorgeous wise,
lie place his ghost amongst the Hierarchies:
For as one starre another far exceeds,
So soules in heauen are placed by their deeds.

With that me thought within her golden lap,
(This Sun-bright Goddesse smiling with her eie,)
The soule of Hatton curiously did wrap,
And in a cloud was taken vp on hie.
Vaine Dreames are fond, but thus as then dreamt I,
And more me thought I heard the Angels sing
An Alleluia for to welcome him.

As thus attendant faire Astrea flew,
The Nobles, Commons, yea and euerie wight,
That liuing in his life time Hatton knew,
Did deepe lament the losse of that good Knight:
But when Astrea was quite out of sight,
For griefe the people shouted such a screame:
That I awooke and start out of my dreame.

I

VERSES AGAINST THE GENTLEWOMEN OF SICILLIA

Since Ladie milde (too base in aray) hath liude as an exile,
None of account but stout: if plaine? state slut not a courtresse
Dames nowadayes? fie none: if not new guised in all points
Fancies fine, sawst with conceits, quick wits verie wilie.
Words of a Saint, but deedes gesse how, fainde faith to deceiue men.

Courtsies coy, no vale but a vaunt trickt vp like a Tuscan.
Paced in print, braue loftie lookes, not vsde with the vestals.
In hearts too glorious, not a glaunce but fit for an Empresse.
As mindes most valorous, so strange in aray: mary stately.
Vp fro the wast like a man, new guise to be casde in a dublet.

Downe to the foote (perhaps like a maid) but hosde to the kneestead.
Some close breetcht to the crotch for cold, tush; peace, tis a shame Syr,
Haires by birth as blacke as let, what? art can amend them.
A perywig frounst fast to the frunt, or curld with a bodkin.
Hats from Fraunce thicke pearld for pride, and plumde like a peacocke.

Ruffes of a syse, stiffe starcht to the necke, of Lawne; mary lawlesse.
Gownes of silke, why those be too bad side, wide with a witnesse.
Small and gent V the wast, but backs as broade as a Burgesse.
Needelesse noughts, as crisps, and scarphes worne h la Morisco.
Fumde with sweetes, as sweete as chast, no want but abundance.

II

ARBASTO'S SONG

Whereat erewhile I wept, I laugh,
That which I feared, I now despise
My victor once, my vassall is,
My fo constrainde, my weale supplie.
Thus doo I triumph on my fo,
I weepe at weale, I laugh at wo.

My care is cur'd, yet hath none ende,
Not that I want, but that I haue,

My chance was change, yet still I stay,
I would haue iesse, and yet I craue:
Ay me poore wretch that thus doe Hue,
Constraind to take, yet forst to giue.

Shee whose delights are signes of Death,
Who when she smiles, begins to lower.
Constant in this that still she change,
Hir sweetest giftes tyme proues but sowre.
I liue in care, crost with hir guile,
Through hir I weepe, at hir I smile.

III

DORALICIA'S SONG

In tyme we see that siluer drops
The craggy stones make soft:
The slowest snaile in tyme, we see,
Doth creepe and clime aloft.

With feeble puffes the tallest pine
In tract of time doth fall:
The hardest hart in time doth yeeld
To Venus luring call.

Where chilling frost alate did nip,
There flasheth now a fire:
Where deepe disdaine bred noisome hate,
There kindleth now desire.

Time causeth hope to haue his hap,
What care in time not easde?
In time I loathd that now I loue,
In both content and pleasd.

IV

THE DESCRIPTION OF SILVESTROS LADIE

Her stature like the tall straight Cedar trees,
Whose stately bulkes doth fame th' Arabian groues,
A pace like princelie Iuno when she braued;
The Queene of Loue fore Paris in the Vale,

A front beset with Loue and Courtesie,
A face like modest Pallas when she blusht:
A seelie shepeheard should be beauties Iudge:
A lip swete ruby red grac'd with delight,
A cheeke wherein for interchaunge of hue,
A wrangling strife twixt Lyllie and the Rose,
Her eyes two tinckling starres in winter nights,
When chilling frost doth cleare the azurd skye:
Her haire of golden hue doth dim the beames,
That proud Apollo giueth from his coach:
The Gnydian doues whose white and snowie pens,
Doth staine the siluer streaming Iuory,
May not compare with those two moiling hils,
Which topt with prettie teates discouers down a vale
Wherein the God of loue may daigne to sleepe:
A foot like Thetis, when she tript the sands,
To steale Neptunes fauor with his steps.
In fine a peece despight of Beautie framde,
To shew what Natures linage could affoorde.

V

LACENAS RIDDLE

The man whose methode hangeth by the Moone, and rules his diot by Geometrie:
Whose restles mind rips up his mothers brest to part her bowels for his familie.
And fetcheth Plutoes glee in fro the grasse, by carelesse cutting of a goddesse gifts:
That throwes his gotten labour to the earth, as trusting to content for others shifts.
Tis he good Sir that Saturne best did please, when golden world set worldlings all at ease.
His name is Person, and his progenie
Now tell me of what auncient petigree.

VI

VERSES VNDER A PICTVRE OF FORTVNE

The fickle seat whereon proud Fortune sits,
the restles globe whereon the furie stands,
Bewraies her fond and farre inconstant fits,
the fruitfull home she handleth in her hands;
Bids all beware to feare her flattering smiles,
that giueth most when most she meaneth guiles.
The wheele that turning neuer taketh rest,
the top whereof fond worldlings count their blisse,

Within a minute makes a blacke exchaunge:
and then the vild and lowest better is:
Which embleme tels vs the inconstant state,
of such as trust to Fortune or to Fate.

VII

A SONNET

The sweete content that quiets angrie thought:
The pleasing sound of howshold harmonie:
The Phisicke that alayes what furie wrought:
The huswifes meanes to make true melodie,
Is not with Simple, Harpe or worldly pelfe,
But smoothly by submitting of her selfe.
Iuno the Queene and mistresse of the skye,
When angry Ioue did threat her with a frowne,
Causde Gamynede for Nectar fast to hye
With pleasing face to wash such cholier downe:
For angry Husbands Andes the soonest ease,
When sweete submission cholier doth appease.
The Lawrell that impales the head with praise,
The Iemme that decks the breast of Iuorie:
The pearle thats orient in her siluer raies:
The Crowne that honors Dames with dignitie:
No Saphier, gold, greene Bayes nor margarit,
But due obedience worketh this delight.

VIII

BARMENISSAS SONG

The stately state that wise men count their good:
The chiefest blisse that luls asleepe desire;
Is not dissent from kings and princely blood:
Ne stately Crowne ambition doth require.
        For birth by fortune is abased downe,
        And perrils are comprisde within a Crowne.

The Scepter and the glittering pompe of mace,
The head impalde with honour and renowne,
The Kingly throne, the seate and regall place,
Are toyes that fade when angrie fortune frowne.
        Content is farre from such delights as those,

Whom woe and daunger doe enuy as foes.

The Cottage seated in the hollowe dale,
That fortune neuer feares, because so lowe:
The quiet mynd that want doth set to sale,
Sleepes safe when Princes seates do ouerthrowe.
      Want smyles secure, when princely thoughts do feele
      That feare and daunger treads vpon their heele.

Blesse fortune thou whose frowne hath wrought thy good:
Bid farewell to the Crowne that ends thy care,
The happie fates thy sorrowes haue withstood,
By syning want and pouertie thy share.
      For now content (fond fortune to despight)
      With patience lows thee quiet and delight.

IX

TEMPORA MVTANTVR, ET NOS MVTAMVR IN ILLIS

Aspyring thoughts led Phaeton amisse,
Proude Icarus did fall he soard so hie:
Seeke not to clymbe with fond Semyramis,
Least Sonne reuenge the fathers iniurie.
      Take heede, Ambition is a sugred ill
      That fortune layes, presumptuous mynds to spill.

The bitter griefe that frets the quiet minde:
The sting that pricks the froward man to woe
Is Enuie, which in honor seld we finde,
And yet to honor sworne a secret foe.
      Learne this of me, enuie not others state,
      The fruites of enuie is enuie and hate.

The mistie Clowde that so eclipseth fame,
That gets reward a Chaos of despight,
Is blacke reuenge which euer winneth shame,
A furie vyld thats hatched in the night.
      Beware, seeke not reuenge against thy foe,
      Least once reuenge thy fortune ouergoe.

These biasing Commets do foreshew mishap,
Let not their flaming lights offend thyne eye
Looke ere thou leape, preuent an after clap:
These three forewarnd well mayst thou flye.
      If now by choyce thou aymest at happie health,

X

VERSES WRITTEN VNDER THE PROTRAITVRE OF VENVS

When Nature forged the faire vnhappy mould,
Wherein proud beauty tooke her matchlesse shape:
She ouer-slipt her cunning and her skill,
And aym'd to faire, but drew beyond the marke;
For thinking to haue made a heauenly blisse,
For wanton gods to dally with in heauen,
And to haue fram'd a precious iem for men,
To solace all their dumpish thoughts with glee,
Shee wrought a plague, a poyson, and a hell
For gods, for men; thus no way wrought she well.
Venus was faire, faire was the queene of loue,
Fairer then Pallas, or the wife of loue:
Yet did the Gigglets beauty greeue the Smith,
For that she brau'd the Creeple with a home.
Mars said, her beauty was the starre of heauen,
Yet did her beauty staine him with disgrace:
Paris for faire, gaue her the golden ball;
And bought his, and his fathers ruine so:
Thus nature making what should farre excell,
Lent gods, and men, a poison and a hell.

XI

VERSES VNDER A PEACOCKE POVRTRAIED. HER LEFT HAND

The bird of Iuno glories in his plumes,
Pride makes the Fowle to prune his feathers sq,
His spotted traine, fetcht from old Argus head,
With golden rayes, like to the brightest sunne;
Inserteth selfe-loue in a silly bird,
Till midst his hot an glorious fumes,
He spies his feete, and then lets fall his plumes.
Beauty breeds pride, pride hatch eth forth disdaine,
Disdaine gets hate, and hate calls for reuenge,
Reuenge with bitter prayers vrgeth still: ia
Thus selfe-loue nursing vp the pompe of pride,
Makes beautie wracke against an ebbing tide.

VERSES VNDER A CARVING OF MERCVRY THROWING FEATHERS INTO THE WINDE.

The richest gift the wealthy heauen affords,
The pearle of price sent from immortall Ioue,
The shape wherein we most resemble gods,
The fire Prometheus stole from lofty skies:
This gift, this pearle, this shape, this fire is it,
Which makes vs men bold by the name of wit.
By wit we search diuine aspect aboue,
By wit we learne what secrets science yeelds,
By wit we speake, by wit the mind is rul'd,
By wit we gouerne all our actions:
Wit is the Load-starre of each humane thought,
Wit is the toole, by which all things are wrought.
The brightest Iacynth hot becommeth darke,
Of little steeme is Crystall being crackt,
Fine heads that can conceit no good, but ill,
Forge oft that breedeth ruine to themselues:
Ripe wits abus'd that build on bad desire,
Do burne themselues like flyes within the fire.

XIII

VERSES VNDER A CARVING OF CVPID BLOWING BLADDERS IN THE AYRE

Loue is a locke that linketh noble mindes,
Faith is the key that shuts the spring of loue,
Lightnesse a wrest, that wringeth all awry,
Lightnesse a plague, that fancie cannot brooke:
Lightnesse in loue, so bad and base a thing,
As foule disgrace to greatest states do bring.

XIV

VERSES ON TWO TABLES HVNG BESIDE AN EFFIGY ON A TOMBE

First Table
The Graces in their glorie neuer gaue
A rich or greater good to womankind:
That more impairs their honors with the Palme,

Of high renowne then matchlesse constancie.
Beauty is vaine, accounted but a flowre,
Whose painted hiew fades with the summer sunne:
Wit oft hath wracke by selfe-conceit of pride.
Riches is trash that fortune boasteth on.
Constant in loue who tries a womans minde,
Wealth, beautie, wit, and all in her doth find.

Second Table
The fairest Iem oft blemish t with a cracke,
Loscth his beauty and his vertue too;
The fairest flowre nipt with the winters frost,
In shew seemes worser then the basest weede.
Vertues are oft farre ouerstain'd with faults,
Were she as faire as Phoebe in her sphere,
Or brighter then the paramour of Mars,
Wiser then Pallas daughter vnto loue,
Of greater maiestie then Iuno was,
More chaste then Vesta goddesse of the Maides,
Of greater faith then faire Lucretia:
Be she a blab, and tattles what she heares,
Want to be secret giues farre greater staines,
Then vertues glorie which in her remaines.

XV

MADRIGALL

Rest thee desire, gaze not at such a Starre,
Sweet fancy sleepe, loue take a nappe awhile:
Thy busie thoughts thatrreach and rome so farre,
With pleasant dreames the length of time beguile.
Faire Venus coole my ouer-heated brest,
And let my fancy take her wonted rest.
Cupid abroad was lated in the night:
His wings were wet with ranging in the raine:
Harbour he sought, to me he tooke his flight,
To drie his plumes: I heard the boy complaine,
My doore I oped to grant him his desire,
And rose my selfe to make the Wagge a fire.
Looking more narrow by the fires flame,
I spyed his quiuer hanging at his backe:
I fear'd the child might my misfortune frame,
I would haue gone for feare of further wracke;
And what I drad (poore man) did me betide,
For foorth he drew an arrow from his side.

He pierst the quicke that I began to start,
The wound was sweete, but that it was too hie,
And yet the pleasure had a pleasing smart:
This done, he flyes away, his wings were drie,
But left his arrow still within my brest,
That now I greeue, I welcom'd such a ghest.

XVI

BRADAMANT'S MADRIGALE

The Swans whose pens as white as Iuory,
Eclipsing fayre Endymions siluer-loue:
Floting like snowe downe by the banckes of Po.
Nere tund their notes like Leda once forlorne:
With more dispairing sortes of madrigales,
Then I whome wanton loue hath with his gad,
Prickt to the courte of deepe and restlesse thoughts.
The frolike yoongsters Bacchus liquor mads,
Run not about the wood of Thessaly,
With more inchaunted fits of lunacy,
Then I whome loue, whome sweete and bitter loue,
Fiers infects with sundry passions,
Now lorne with liking ouermuch my loue,
Frozen with fearing, if I step to far:
Fired with gazing at such glymmering stars,
As stealing light from Phebus brightest rayes.
Sparkles and sets a flame within my brest,
Rest restlesse Loue, fond baby be content:
Child hold thy darts within thy quiuer close;
And if thou wilt be rouing with thy bowe,
Ayme at those hearts that may attend on loue,
Let countrey swaines, and silly swads be still,
To Court yoong wag, and wanton there thy fill.

XVII

MELISSA'S DITTYE

Obscure and darke is all the gloomie aire,
The curtaine of the night is ouerspred:
The sylent Mistresse of the lowest spheare,
Puts on her sable coulored vale and lower.
Nor Star nor Milkewhite cyrcle of the skye

Appeares where discontent doth hold her lodge.
She sits shrind in a Cannapie of Clouds,
Whose massie darkenesse mazeth euery sense,
Wan is her lookes, her cheekes of Azure hue,
Hir haires as gorgons foule retorting snakes,
Enuie the glasse wherein the hag doth gaze,
Restlesse the clocke that chimes hir fast a sleepe,
Disquiet thoughts the minuts of her watch,
Forth from her Caue the fiend full oft dooth flie,
To Kings she goes, and troubles them with Crownes,
Setting those high aspiring brands on fire,
That flame from earth vnto the seate of loue,
To such as Midas, men that dote on wealth,
And rent the bowels of the middle earth:
For come: who gape, as did faire Danae,
For showers of gold their discontent in blacke,
Throwes forth the viols of her restlesse cares,
To such as sit at Paphos for releefe,
And offer Venus manie solemne vowes,
To such as Hymen in his saffron robe,
Hath knit a Gordion knot of passions,
To these, to all, parting the glonne aire,
Black discontent doth make hir bad repaire.

XVIII

PRINCE'S SONNET

In Cypres sat fayre Venus by a Fount,
Wanton Adonis toying on her knee,
She kist the wag, her darling of accompt,
The Boie gan blush, which when his louer see,
> She smild and told him loue might challenge debt,
> And he was yoong and might be wanton yet.

The boy waxt bold fiered by fond desire,
That woe he could, and court hir with conceipt,
Reason spied this, and sought to quench the fire
With cold disdaine, but wily Adon straight
> Cherd vp the flame and saide good sir what let,
> I am but young and may be wanton yet.

Reason replied that Beawty was a bane
To such as feed their fancy with fond loue,
That when sweete youth with lust is ouertane,
It rues in age, this could not Adon moue,

For Venus taught him still this rest to set
That he was young, and might be wanton yet.

Where Venus strikes with Beauty to the quick,
It litle vayles sage reason to reply:
Few are the cares for such as are loue-sicke
But loue: then though I wanton it awry
     And play the wag: from Adon this I get,
     I am but young >and may be wanton yet.

XIX

SONNET OF OLDE MAN (A CALDEE) IN ANSWER

The Syren Venus nourist in hir lap
Faire Adon, swearing whiles he was a youth
He might be wanton: Note his after-hap
The guerdon that such lawlesse lust ensueth,
     So long he followed flattering Venus lore,
     Till seely Lad, he perisht by a bore.

Mars in his youth did court this lusty dame
He woon hir loue, what might his fancy let
He was but young: at last vnto his shame
Vulcan intrapt them slily in a net,
     And call'd the Gods to witnesse as a truth,
     A leachers fault was not excus'd by youth.

If crooked Age accounteth youth his spring;
The spring, the fayrest season of the yeare,
Enricht with flowers and sweetes, and many a thing
That fayre and gorgeous to the eyes appeare:
     It fits that youth the spring of man should be,
     Richt with such flowers as vertue yeeldeth thee.

XX

SONNET

Faire is my loue for Aprill in her face,
Hir louely brests September claimes his part,
And Lordly Iuly in her eyes takes place,
But colde December dwelleth in her heart:
     Blest be the months, that sets my thoughts on fire,

Accurst that Month that hindreth my desire.

Like Phoebus fire, so sparkles both her eies,
As ayre perfumde with Amber is her breath:
Like swelling waues her louely teates do rise,
As earth hir heart, cold, dateth me to death.
      Aye me poore man that on the earth do liue,
      When vnkind earth, death and dispaire doth giue.

In pompe sits Mercie seated in hir face,
Loue twixt her brests his trophees dooth imprint.
Her eyes shines fauour, courtesie, and grace:
But touch her heart, ah that is framd of flynt;
      That fore my haruest in the Grasse beares graine,
      The rockt will weare, washt with a winters raine.

XXI

SONNET

Phillis kept sheepe along the westerne plaines,
And Coridon did feed his flocks hard by:
This Sheepheard was the flower of all the swaines,
That trac'd the downes of fruitfull Thessalie,
      And Phillis that did far her flocks surpasse,
      In siluer hue was thought a bonny lasse.

A Bonny lasse quaint in her Country tire,
Was louely Phillis, Coridon swore so:
Her locks, her lookes, did set the swaine on fire,
He left his Lambes, and he began to woe,
      He lookt, he sitht, he courted with a kisse:
      No better could the silly swad then this.

He little knew to paint a tale of Loue;
Sheepheards can fancie, but they cannot saye:
Phillis gan smile, and wily thought to proue,
What vncouth greefe poore Coridon did paie,
      She askt him how his flocks or he did fare,
      Yet pensiue thus his sighes did tell his care.

The sheepheard blusht when Phillis questioned so,
And swore by Pan it was not for his flocke:
Tis loue faire Phillis breedeth all this woe:
My thoughts are trapt within thy louely locks,
      Thine eye hath pearst, thy face hath set on fire.

Faire Phillis kindleth Coridons desire.

Can sheepheards loue, said Phillis to the swaine,
Such saints as Phillis, Coridon replied:
Then when they lust, can many fancies faine,
Said Phillis: this not Coridon denied:
      That lust had lies, but loue quoth he sayes truth.
      Thy sheepheard loues, then Phillis what ensueth.

Phillis was wan, she blusht and hung the head,
The swaine stept to, and cher'd hir with a kisse,
With faith, with troth, they stroke the matter dead,
So vsed they when men thought not amisse;
      This Loue begun and ended both in one,
      Phillis was loued, and she lik't Corydon.

XXII

BELLARIA'S EPITAPH

Here lyes entombde Bellaria faire.
Falsly accused to be vnchaste:
Cleared by Apollos sacred doome,
Yet slaine by Iealousie at last.
What ere thou bee that passeth by,
Cursse him that causde this Queene to die.

XXIII

Dorastus (in Loue-passion) writes these lines in Praise of his louing and best-beloued Fawnia.

Ah! were she pitiful as she is fair,
Or but as mild as she is seeming so,
Then were my hopes greater than my despair;
Then all the World were Heauen, nothing Woe.
Ah! were her Heart relenting as her Hand,
That seems to melt e'en with the mildest touch,
Then knew I where to seat me in a Land
Vnder the wide Heauens, but yet not such:
Iust as she shews, so seems the budding Rose,
Yet sweeter far than is an earthly Flower;
Soueraign of Beauty! like the spray she grows,
Compass'd she is with Thorns and canker'd bower:
Yet where she willing to be pluck'd and worn,

She would be gathered, tho' she grew on Thorn.
Ah! when she sings, all Musick else be still,
For none must be compared to her Note;
Ne'er breath'd such Glee from Philomela's Bill;
Nor from the Morning Singer's swelling Throat,
Ah! when she riseth from her blissful Bed,
She comforts all the World, as doth the Sun;
And at her sight the Nights foul Vapours fled,
When she is set, the gladsom Day is done:
O Glorious Sun! imagine me the West,
Shine in my Arms, and set thou in my Breast.

XXIV

APOLLO'S ORACLE (DOOME)

When Neptune riding on the Southerne seas
Shall from the bosome of his Lemman yeeld
Th' arcadian wonder, men and Gods to please:
Plentie in pride shall march amidst the field,
Dead men shall warre, and vnborne babes shall frowne,
And with their fawchens hew their foemen downe.
When Lambes haue Lions for their surest guide,
And Planets rest vpon th' arcadian hills:
When swelling seas haue neither ebbe nor tide,
When equall bankes the Ocean margine fills.
Then looke Arcadians for a happie time,
And sweete content within your troubled clyme.

XXV

MENAPHON'S SONG

Some say Loue
Foolish Loue
        Doth rule and gouerne all the Gods,
I say Loue,
Inconstant Loue
        Sets mens senses farre at ods.
Some sweare Loue
Smooth'd face Loue
        Is sweetest sweete that men can haue:
I say Loue,
Sower Loue

Makes vertue yeeld as beauties slaue.
A bitter sweete, a follie worst of all
That forceth wisedome to be follies thrall
Loue is sweete,
Wherein sweete?
     In fading pleasures that doo paine.
Beautie sweete.
Is that sweete
     That yeeldeth sorrow for a gaine?
If Loues sweete,
Heerein sweete
     That Minutes ioyes are monthlie woes.
Tis not sweete,
That is sweete
     Nowhere, but where repentance growes.
Then loue who list if beautie be so sower:
Labour for me, Loue rest in Princes bower.

XXVI

SEPHESTIAS SONG TO HER CHILDE

Weepe not my wanton smile vpon my knee,
When thou art olde ther's griefe inough for thee.
     Mothers wagge, pretie boy,
     Fathers sorrow, fathers joy.
     When thy father first did see
     Such a boy by him and mee,
     He was glad, I was woe,
     Fortune changde made him so,
     When he left his pretie boy,
     Last his sorrowe, first his ioy.
Weepe not my wanton smile vpon my knee:
When thou art olde ther's griefe inough for thee.
     Streaming teares that neuer stint,
     Like pearle drops from a flint
     Fell by course from his eyes,
     That one anothers place supplies:
     Thus he grieud in euerie part,
     Teares of bloud fell from his hart,
     When he left his pretie boy,
     Fathers sorrow, fathers joy.
Weepe not my wanton smile vpon my knee:
When thou art olde ther's griefe inough for thee.
     The wanton smilde, father wept:
     Mother cride, babie lept:

More he crowde, more we cride;
Nature could not sorowe hide.
He must goe, he must kisse
Childe and mother, babie blisse:
For he left his pretie boy,
Fathers sorowe, fathers joy,
Weepe not my wanton smile vpon my knee:
When thou art olde ther's griefe inough for thee.

XXVII

MENAPHONS ROVNDELAY

When tender ewes brought home with euening Sunne
Wend to their foldes,
And to their holdes
The shepheards trudge when light of daye is done.
Vpon a tree
The Eagle loues faire bird did pearch,
There resteth bee.
A little flie his harbor then did search,
And did presume (though others laught there at)
To pearch whereas the princelie Eagle sat.
The Eagle frownd, and shooke her royall wings,
And chargde the Flie
From thence to hie.
Afraid in hast the little creature flings,
Yet seekes againe
Fearfull to pearke him by the Eagles side,
With moodie vaine
The speedie post of Ganimede replide;
Vassaile auant or with my wings you die,
Ist fit an Eagle seate him with a Flie?
The Flie craude pitie, still the Eagle frownde,
The sillie Flie
Readie to die
Disgracte, displacte, fell groueling to the ground.
The Eagle sawe
And with a royall minde said to the Flie,
Be not in awe,
I scorne by me the meanest creature die;
Then seate thee heere: the ioyfull Flie vp flings,
And sate safe shadowed with the Eagles wings.

DORON'S DESCRIPTION OF SAMELA.

Like to Diana in her Summer weede
Girt with a crimson roabe of brightest die, goes faire Samela.
Whiter than be the flockes that straggling feede,
When washt by Arethusa's Fount they lie: is faire Samela.
As faire Aurora in her morning gray
Deckt with the ruddie glister of her loue, is faire Samela.
Like louelie Thetis on a calmed day,
When as her brightnesse Neptunes fancie moue, shines faire Samela.
Her tresses gold, her eyes like glassie streames,
Her teeth are pearle, the breasts are yuorie of faire Samela.
Her cheekes like rose and lilly yeeld foorth gleames,
Her browes bright arches framde of ebonie:
Thus faire Samela.
Passeth faire Venus in her brauest hiew,
And Iuno in the shew of maiestie, for she's Samela.
Pallas in wit, all three if you well view,
For beautie, wit, and matchlesse dignitie yeeld to Samela.

XXIX

DORONS IIGGE

Through the shrubbes as I can cracke,
        For my Lambes little ones,
        Mongst many pretie ones,
Nimphes I meane, whose haire was blacke
            As the crow:
            Like the snow
Her face and browes shinde I weene:
        I saw a little one,
        A bonny prety one,
As bright, buxsome and as sheene
            As was shee.
            On hir knee
That lulld the God, whose arrowes warmes
        Such merry little ones,
        Such faire fac'd prety ones,
As dally in Loues chiefest harmes,
            Such was mine:
            Whose gray eyne
Made me loue. I gan to woo
        This sweete little one,

This bonny pretie one.
I wooed hard a day or two,
                 Till she bad:
                 Be not sad,
Wooe no more I am thine owne,
                 Thy dearest little one,
                 Thy truest pretie one:
Thus was faith and firme loue shownc,
                 As behoues
                 Shepheards loues.

XXX

MELICERTVS MADRIGALE

What are my sheepe without their wonted food?
What is my life except I gaine my Loue?
My sheepe consume and faint for want of blood.
My life is lost vnlesse I grace approue.
                 No flower that saplesse thriues:
                 No turtle without pheare.

The day without the Sunne dooth lowre for woe,
Then woe mine eyes vnlesse they beautie see;
My Sunne Samelaes eyes, by whom I know
Wherein delight consists, where pleasures be,
                 Nought more the heart reuiues
                 Than to imbrace his deare.

The starres from earthly humors gaine their light,
Our humors by their light possesse their power:
Samelaes eyes fedde by my weeping sight,
Insues my paine or ioyes by smile, or lower.
                 So wends the source of loue.
                 It feedes, it fades, it ends.

Kinde lookes cleare to your ioy behold her eyes,
Admire her heart, desire to taste her kisses;
In them the heauen of ioy and solace lies,
Without them euery hope his succour misses,
                 Oh how I loue to prooue.
                 Wheretoo this solace tends.

XXXI

MENAPHON'S SONG IN HIS BEDDE

You restlesse cares companions of the night,
That wrap my ioyes in folds of endlesse woes:
Tyre on my heart, and wound it with your spight,
Since Loue and Fortune proues my equall foes.
      Farewell my hopes, farewell my happic daies:
      Welcome sweete griefe, the subiect of my laies.

Mourne heauens, mourne earth, your shepheard is forlorne;
Mourne times and houres since bale inuades my bowre:
Curse euerie tongue the place where I was borne,
Curse euerie thought the life which makes me lowre.
      Farewell my hopes, farewell my happic daies,
      Welcome sweete griefe the subiect of my laies.

Was I not free? was I not fancies aime?
Framde not desire my face to front disdaine?
I was; she did: but now one silly maime
Makes me to droope as he whom loue hath slaine.
      Farewell my hopes, farewell my happie daies,
      Welcome sweete griefe the subiect of my layes.

Yet drooping, and yet liuing to this death,
I sigh, I sue for pitie at her shrine,
Whose fierie eyes exhale my vitall breath,
And make my flockes with parching heate to pine.
      Farewell my hopes, farewell my happie daies,
      Welcome sweete griefe the subiect of my layes.

Fade they, die I, long may she liue to blisse
That feedes a wanton fire with fuell of her forme,
And makes perpetuall summer where shee is;
Whiles I doo crie oretooke with enuies storme,
      Farewell my hopes, farewell my happie daies:
      Welcome sweete griefe, the subiect of my laies.

XXXII

MENAPHON'S DITTIE

Faire fields proud Floras vaunt, why is't you smile
                  when as I languish?
You golden meads, why striue you to beguile
                  my weeping anguish?

I liue to sorrow, you to pleasure spring:
                            why doo you spring thus?
What will not Boreas tempests wrathfull king
                            take some pitie on vs?
And send foorth Winter in hir rustie weede,
                            to waile my bemonings;
Whiles I distrest doo tune my countrey reede
                            vnto my gronings.
But heauen, and earth, time, place, and euerie power
                            haue with her conspired
To turne my blisse full sweetes to bale full sower,
                            Since fond I desired
The heauen whereto my thoughts may not aspire:
                            ay me vnhappie.
It was my fault and imbrace my bane the fire
                            that forceth me die.
Mine be the paine, but hirs the cruell cause
                            of this strange torment:
Wherefore no time my banning praiers shall pause,
                            till proud she repent.

XXXIII

MENAPHONS ECLOGVE

Too weake the wit, too slender is the braine
That meanes to marke the power and worth of loue;
Not one that hues (except he hap to proue)
Can tell the sweete, or tell the secret paine.

Yet I that haue been prentice to the griefe,
Like to the cunning sea-man from a farre,
By gesse will take the beautie of that starre,
Whose influence must yeeld the chiefe reliefe.

You censors of the glorie of my deare,
With reuerence and lowlie bent of knee,
Attend and marke what her perfections bee:
For in my words my fancies shall appeare.

Hir lockes are pleighted like the fleece of wooli
That Iason with his Gretian mates atchiude,
As pure as golde, yet not from golde deriude;
As full of sweetes, as sweete of sweetes is full.

Her browes are pretie tables of conceate,

Where Loue his records of delight dooth quoate,
On them her dallying lockes doo daily floate
As Loue full oft dooth feede vpon the baite.

Her eyes, faire eyes, like to the purest lights
That animate the Sunne, or cheere the day,
In whom the shining Sun-beames brightly play
Whiles fancie dooth on them diuine delights.

Hir cheekes like ripened lillies steept in wine,
Or faire pomegranade kernels washt in milke,
Or snow white threds in nets of crimson silke,
Or gorgeous cloudes vpon the Sunnes decline.

Her lips are roses ouerwasht with dew,
Or like the purple of Narcissus flower:
No frost their faire, no winde doth wast their power,
But by her breath her beauties doo renew.

Hir christall chin like to the purest molde,
Enchac'de with daintie daysies soft and white,
Where fancies faire pauilion once is pight,
Whereas imbrac'de his beauties he doth holde.

Hir necke like to an yuorie shining tower
Where through with azure veynes sweete Nectar runnes,
Or like the downe of swannes where Senesse woons,
Or like delight that doth it selfe deuoure.

Hir pappes are like faire apples in the prime,
As round as orient pearles, as soft as downe:
They neuer vaile their faire through winters frowne,
But from their sweetes Loue suckt his summer time.

Hir bodie beauties best esteemed bowre,
Delicious, comely, daintie, without staine:
The thought whereof (not touch) hath wrought my paine.
Whose faire, all faire and beauties doth deuoure,

Hir maiden mount, the dwelling house of pleasure;
Not like, for why no like surpasseth wonder:
O blest is he may bring such beauties vnder,
Or search by sute the secrets of that treasure.

Deuourd in thought, how wanders my deuice,
What rests behind I must deuine vpon?
Who talkes the best, can say but fairer none:
Few words well coucht doo most content the wise.

All you that heare; let not my sillie stile
Condemne my zeale: for what my tongue should say
Serues to inforce my thoughts to seeke the way
Whereby my woes and cares I doo beguile.

Selde speaketh Loue, but sighs his secret paines;
Teares are his truceman, words doo make him tremble.
How sweete is loue to them that can dissemble
In thoughts and lookes, till they haue reapt the gaines,

Alonely I complaine, and what I say
I thinke, yet what I thinke tongue cannot tell:
Sweete censors take my silly worst for well:
My faith is firme, though homely be my laye.

XXXIV

MELICERTVS ECLOGVE

What neede compare where sweete exceedes compare?
Who drawes his thoughts of loue from senselesse things,
Their pompe and greatest glories doth impaire,
And mounts Loues heauen with ouer leaden wings.

Stones, hearbes and flowers, the foolish spoyles of earth,
Flouds, mettalls, colours, dalliance of the eye:
These shew conceipt is staind with too much dearth:
Such abstract fond compares make cunning die.

But he that hath the feeling taste of Loue
Deriues his essence from no earthlie toy;
A weake conceipt his power cannot approue,
For earthly thoughts are subiect to annoy.

Be whist, be still, be silent Censers now;
My fellow swaine has tolde a pretie tale
Which moderne Poets may perhaps allow,
Yet I condemne the tearmes; for they are stale.

Apollo when my Mistres first was borne
Cut off his lockes, and left them on hir head,
And said; I plant these wires in Natures scorne,
Whose beauties shall appeare when Time is dead.

From foorth the christall heauen when she was made,

The puritie thereof did taint hir brow:
On which the glistering Sunne that sought the shade
Gan set, and there his glories doth auow,

Those eyes, faire eyes, too faire to be describde,
Were those that earst the chaos did reforme:
To whom the heauen their beauties haue ascribde,
That fashion life in man, in beast, in worme.

When first hir faire delicious cheekes were wrought,
Aurora brought hir blush, the Moone hir white:
Both so combinde as passed Natures thought,
Compilde those pretie orbes of sweete delight.

When Loue and Nature once were proud with play,
From both their lips hir lips the corail drew:
On them doth fancy sleepe, and euerie day
Doth swallow ioy such sweete delights to view.

Whilome while Venus Sonne did seeke a bowre
To sport with Psyche his desired deare,
He chose her chinne; and from that happie stowre
He neuer stints in glorie to appeare.

Desires and Ioyes that long had serued Loue,
Besought a Holde where pretie eyes might woo them:
Loue made her neeke, and for their best behoue
Hath shut them there, whence no man can vndoo them.

Once Venus dreamt vpon two pretie things,
Hir thoughts they were affections chiefest neasts:
She suckt and sightht, and bathde hir in the springs,
And when she wakt they were my Mistres breasts.

Once Cupide sought a holde to couch his kisses,
And found the bodie of my best beloude.
Wherein he closde the beautie of his blisses,
And from that bower can neuer be remoude.

The graces earst, when Acidalian springs
Were waxen drie, perhaps did finde hir fountaine
Within the vale of blisse, where cupides wings
Doo shield the Nectar fleeting from the mountaine.

No more fond man: things infinite I see
Brooke no dimension: Hell a foolish speech;
For endles things may neuer talked be.
Then let me liue to honor and beseech.

Sweete natures pompe, if my deficient phraze
Hath staind thy glories by too little skill,
Yeeld pardon though mine eye that long did gaze,
Hath left no better patterne to my quill.

I will no more, no more will I detaine
Your listning eares with dallyance of my tongue:
I speake my ioyes; but yet conceale my paine;
My paine too olde, although my yeres be yong.

XXXV

DORONS ECLOGVE IOYND WITH CARMELAS

Sit downe Carmela here are cobs for kings,
Slowes blacke as ieat, or like my Christmas shooes,
Sweete Sidar which my leathren bottle brings;
Sit downe Carmela let me kisse thy toes.

Carmela
Ah Doron, ah my heart, thou art as white,
As is my mothers Calfe or brinded Cow,
Thine eyes are like the glow-wormes in the night,
Thine haires resemble thickest of the snow.

The lines within thy face are deepe and cleere
Like to the furrowes of my fathers waine,
Thy sweate vpon thy face dooth oft appeare
Like to my mothers fat and kitchin gaine.

Ah leaue my toe and kisse my lippes my loue,
My lippes and thine, for I haue giuen them thee:
Within thy cap tis thou shalt weare my gloue,
At foote ball sport thou shalt my champion be.

Doron
Carmela deare, euen as the golden ball
That Venus got, such are thy goodly eyes,
When cherries iuice is iumbled therewithall,
Thy breath is like the steeme of apple pies.

Thy lippes resemble two Cowcumbers faire,
Thy teeth like to the tuskes of fattest swine,
Thy speach is like the thunder in the aire:
Would God thy toes, thy lips and all were mine.

Carmela

Doron what thing dooth mooue this wishing griefe.

Doron

Tis Loue Carmela ah tis cruell Loue.
That like a slaue, and caitiffe villaine thiefe,
Hath cut my throate of ioy for thy behoue.

Carmela

Where was he borne?

Doron

In faith I know not where.
But I haue heard much talking of his dart.
Ay me poore man, with manie a trampling teare,
I feele him wound the forehorse of my heart,

What doo I loue? O no, I doo but talke.
What shall I die for loue? O no, not so.
What am I dead? O no my tongue dooth walke.
Come kisse Carmela, and confound my woe.

Carmela

Euen with this kisse, as once my father did,
I seale the sweete indentures of delight:
Before I breake my vowe the Gods forbid,
No not by day, nor yet by darkesome night.

Doron

Euen with this garland made of Holly-hocks
I crosse thy browes from euerie shepheerds kisse.
Heigh hoe how glad am I to touch thy lockes,
My frolicke heart euen now a free man is.

Carmela

I thanke you Doron, and will thinke on you,
I loue you Doron, and will winke on you.
I seale your charter pattent with my thummes,
Come kisse and part for feare my mother comes.

XXXVI

SONETTO

What thing is Loue? It is a power diuine

That raines in vs: or else a wreakefull law
That doomes our mindes to beautie to encline:
It is a starre whose influence dooth draw
    Our hearts to Loue dissembling of his might,
    Till he be master of our hearts and sight.

Loue is a discord and a strange diuorce
Betwixt our sense and reason, by whose power
As madde with reason we admit that force,
Which wit or labour neuer may deuoure,
    It is a will that brooketh no consent:
    It would refuse, yet neuer may repent.

Loue's a desire, which for to waite a time,
Dooth loose an age of yeeres, and so doth passe
As dooth the shadow seuerd from his prime,
Seeming as though it were, yet neuer was.
    Leauing behinde nought but repentant thoughts
    Of daies ill spent, for that which profits noughts.

Tis now a peace, and then a sodaine warre,
A hope consumde before it is conceiude,
At hand it feares, and menaceth a farre,
And he that gaines is most of all deceiude:
    It is a secret hidden and not knowne,
    Which one may better feele than write vpon.

XXXVII

MELICERTVS DESCRIPTION OF HIS MISTRES

Tune on my pipe the praises of my Loue,
And midst thy oaten harmonie recount
How faire she is that makes thy musicke mount,
And euerie string of thy hearts harpe to moue.

Shall I compare her forme vnto the spheare
Whence Sun-bright Venus vaunts her siluer shine?
Ah more than that by iust compare is thine,
Whose christall lookes the cloudie heauens doe cleare.

How oft haue I descending Titan seene
His burning lockes couch in the Sea-queenes lap,
And beauteous Thetis his red bodie wrap
In watrie roabes, as he her Lord had been.

When as my Nimph impatient of the night
Bad bright Astraeus with his traine giue place,
Whiles she led foorth the day with her faire face,
And lent each starre a more than Delian light.

Not loue or Nature should they both agree
To make a woman of the Firmament,
Of his mixt puritie could not inuent
A Skie borne forme so beautifull as she.

XXXVIII

VERSES FROM CICERONIS AMOR

Wherefore by an auncient Poet were written these verses

When Gods had framd the sweete of womens face,
        and lockt mens lookes within their golden haire:
That Phoebus flusht to see their matchles grace,
        and heauenly Gods on earth did make repaire
        To quippe faire Venus ouer weening pride
        Loues happie thoughts to ielousie were tide.

Then grew a wrinkle on faire Venus browe,
The amber sweete of loue was turnd to gall:
Gloomie was heauen: bright Phoebus did auowe
He could be coy and would not loue at all,
        Swering no greater mischiefe could be wrought
        Then loue vnited to a ielous thought.

XXXIX

POEM

Vita quae tandem magis est iucunda,
Vel viris doctis magis expetenda,
Mente quam pura sociam iugalem,
Semper amare?

Vita quae tandem magis est dolenda,
Vel magis cunctis fugienda, quam quae,
(Falso suspecta probitate amicae)
Tollit amorem?

Nulla earn tollit medicina pestem,
Murmur, emplastrum, vel imago sagae,
Astra nec curant, magicae nec artes,
Zelotypiam.

XL

SONNET OR DITTIE

Mars in a fury gainst loues brightest Queene
    Put on his helme and tooke him to his launce:
On Erecynus mount was Mauors seene,
    And there his ensignes did the god aduance.
        And by heauens greatest gates he stowtly swore,
        Venus should die for she had wrongd him sore,

Cupid heard this and he began to cry,
    And wisht his mothers absence for a while:
Peace, foole, quoth Venus, is it I must die?
    Must it be Mars? with that she coind a smile:
        She trimd hir tresses and did curie hir haire,
        And made hir face with beautie passing faire.

A fan of siluer feathers in hir hand,
    And in a coach of Ebony she went:
She past the place where furious Mars did stand,
    And out hir lookes a louely smile she sent,
        Then from hir browes lept out so sharpe a frowne,
        That Mars for feare threwe all his armour downe.

He vowd repentance for his rash misdeede,
    Blaming his choller that had causd his woe:
Venus grew gratious, and with him agred,
    But chargd him not to threaten beautie so,
        For womens lookes are such inchaunting charmes,
        As can subdue the greatest god in armes.

XLI

RVNDELAY

Fond faining poets make of loue a god,
And leaue the Lawrell for the myrtle boughes:
When Cupid is a child not past the rod,

And faire Diana Daphne most allowes.
lie weare the bayes and call the wag a boy,
And thinke of loue but as a foolish toy.

Some giue him bowe and quiuer at his backe,
Some make him blinde to aime without aduise:
When naked wretch such feathered bolts he lacke,
And sight he hath but cannot wrong the wise.
For vse but labours weapon for defence,
And Cupid like a Coward flieth thence.

He is god in Court but cottage cals him childe,
And Vestas virgins with their holy fires
Doe cleanse the thoughtes that fancie hath defild,
And burnes the pallace of his fonde desires.
With chast disdain they scorne the foolish god;
And prooue him but a boy not past the rod.

XLII

LENTVLVS DESCRIPTION OF TERENTIA IN LATIN

Qualis in aurora splendescit lumine Titan,
Talis in eximio corpore forma fuit:
Lumina seu spectes radiantia, siue capillos,
Lux Ariadne tua et lux tua, Phoebe iacet.
Venustata fuit verbis, spirabat odorem,
Musica vox, nardus, spiritus almus erat:
Rubea labra, genae rubrae, faciesque decora,
In qua concertant lilius atque rosa,
Luxuriant geminae formoso in pectore mammae,
Circundant niueae Candida colla comae: io
Denique talis erat diuina Terentia, quales
Quondam certantes, Iuno, Minerua, Venus.

Thus in English

Brightsome Apollo in his richest pompe,
Was not like to the tramels of hir haire:
Her eies like Ariadnes sparkling starres,
Shone from the Ebon Arches of hir browes.
Hir face was like the blushing of the east,
When Titan chargde the morning Sun to rise:
Hir cheeks rich strewd with roses and with white,
Did stayne the glorie of Anchises loue.
Hir siluer teates did ebbe and flow delight,

Hir necke columme of polisht Iuory.
Hir breath was perfume made of violets,
And all this heauen was but Terentia.

XLIII

THE SHEEPHEARDS ODE

Walking in a valley greene,
Spred with Flora summer queene:
Where shee heaping all hir graces,
Niggard seemd in other places.
Spring it was and here did spring,
All that nature forth can bring:
Groues of pleasant trees there grow,
Which fruite and shadowe could bestow.
Thick leaued boughes small birds couer,
Till sweete notes themselues discouer:
Tunes for number seemd confounded,
Whilst their mixtures musickes sounded,
Greeing well, yet not agreed,
That one the other shoulde exceede.
A swete streame here silent glides,
Whose cleare water no fish hides.
Slow it runes which well bewraid,
The pleasant shore the current staid:
In this streame a rock was planted,
Where no art nor nature wanted.
Each thing so did other grace,
As all places maye giue place.
Onely this the place of pleasure,
Where is heaped nature's treasure.
Heere mine eyes with woonder staid,
Eies amasd and minde afraid:
Rauisht with what was beheld,
From departing were withheld.
Musing then with sound aduise,
On this earthly paradise:
Sitting by the riuer side
Louely Phillis was discrid:
Golde hir haire, bright her eyen,
Like to Phoebus in his shine.
White hir brow, hir face was faire.
Amber breath perfumde the aire.
Rose and Lilly both did seeke,
To shew their glories on hir cheeke.

Loue did nestle in hir lookes.
Baiting there his sharpest hookes.
Such a Phillis nere was seene,
More beautiful than Loues Queene.
Doubt it was whose greater grace,
Phillis beautie or the place.
Hir coate was of scarlet red,
All in pleates a mantle spred:
Fringd with gold, a wreath of bowes.
To checke the sunne from hir browes.
In hir hand a shepheards hooke,
In hir face Dianas looke:
Hir sheepe grased on the plaines,
She had stolne from the swaines.
Vnder a coole silent shade,
By the streames shee garlands made.
Thus sat Phillis all alone,
Mist shee was by Coridon:
Chiefest swaine of all the rest,
Louely Phyllis likt him best.
His face was like Phoebus loue,
His necke white as Venus Doue,
A ruddie cheeke hide with smiles,
Such loue hath when he beguiles.
His lookes browne, his eyes were gray,
Like Titan in a summer day.
A russet Iacket sleeues red,
A blew bonnet on his hed:
A cloake of gray fencst the raine,
Thus tyred was this louely swaine.
A shepheards hooke his dog tide,
Bag and bottle by his side:
Such was Paris shepheards say,
When with Oenone he did play.
From his flocke straide Coridon,
Spying Phillis all alone:
By the streame he Phillis spide,
Brauer then was Floras pride,
Downe the valley gan he tracke:
Stole behinde his true loues backe:
The sunne shone and shadow made
Phillis rose and was afraid.
When shee saw hir louer there,
Smile shee did and left hir feare:
Cupid that disdaine doth loth,
With desire stracke them both.
The swaine did woe, she was nise,
Following fashion nayed him twise:

Much adooe hee kist hir then,
Madens blush when they kisse men:
So did Phillis at that stowre,
Hir face was like the rose flowre.
Last they greed for loue would so,
Faith and troth they would no mo.
For shepheards euer held it sin,
To false the loue they liued in,
The swaine gaue a girdle red,
Shee set garlandes on his hed.
Giftes were giuen, they kisse againe,
Both did smile for both were faine:
Thus was loue mongst shephards solde,
When fancy knew not what was golde:
They woed and vowed, and that they keep,
And goe contented to their sheep.

XLIV

ORPHEVS SONG

He that did sing the motions of the starres,
Pale colour'd Phaebus borrowing of her light:
Aspects of planets oft oppos'd in iarres,
Of Hesper Henchmen to the day and night
        Sings now of Loue as taught by proofe to sing:
        Women are false and loue a bitter thing.

I lou'd Eurydice the brighest Lasse,
More fond to like so faire a Nymph as she:
In Thesaly, so bright none euer was,
But faire and constant hardly may agree.
        False harted wife to him that loued thee well:
        To leaue thy loue and choose the Prince of hell.

Theseus did helpe, and I in hast did hie,
To Pluto, for the Lasse I loued so:
The God made graunt, and who so glad as I,
I tunde my Harpe, and shee and I gan goe,
        Glad that my loue was left to me alone.
        I looked back, Eurydice was gone.

She slipt aside backe to her latest loue,
Vnkinde shee wrong'd her first and truest Feere,
Thus womens loues, delights as tryall proues,
By false Eurydice I loued so deere.

To change, and fleete, and euery way to shrinke,
To take in loue, and lose it with a winke.

XLV

THE SONG OF ARION

Seated vpon the crooked Dolphins back,
Scudding amidst the purple coloured waues:
Gazing aloofe for Land, Neptune in black,
Attended with the Tritons as his slaues.
Threw forth such stormes as made the ayre thick:
For greefe his Lady Thetis was so sick.

Such plaints he throbd as made the Dolphin stay,
Women (quoth he) are harbours of mans health:
Pleasures for night, and comforts for the day,
What are faire women but rich natures wealth.
Thetis is such, and more if more may be:
Thetis is sick, then what may comfort me?

Women are sweets that salue mens sowrest ills,
Women are Saints, their vertues are so rare:
Obedient soules that seeke to please mens wills,
Such loue with faith, such Iewels women are.
Thetis is such, and more if more may be:
Thetis is sick, then what may comfort me?

With that he diu'd into the Corall waues,
To see his loue, with all his watry slaues,
The Dolphin swam, yet this I learned then:
Faire women are rich Iewells vnto men.

XLVI

SONNET

Cupid abroade was lated in the night,
        His winges were wet with ranging in the raine,
Harbour he sought, to mee hee tooke his flight,
        To dry his plumes I heard the boy complaine.
                I opte the doore, and graunted his desire,
                I rose my selfe, and made the wagge a fire.

Looking more narrow by the fiers flame,
    I spied his quiuer hanging by his backe:
Doubting the boy might my misfortune frame,
    I would haue gone for feare of further wrack.
        But what I drad, did me poore wretch betide:
        For forth he drew an arrow from his side.

He pierst the quick, and I began to start,
    A pleasing wound but that it was too hie,
His shaft procurde a sharpe, yet sugred smart,
    Away he flewe, for why his winges were dry.
        But left the arrow sticking in my brest:
        That sore I greeude I welcomd such a guest.

XLVII

THE DESCRIPTION OF THE SHEPHEARD AND HIS WIFE

It was neere a thicky shade,
That broad leaues of Beech had made:
Ioyning all their tops so nie,
That scarce Phoebus in could prie,
To see if Louers in the thicke,
Could dally with a wanton tricke.
Where sate the swaine and his wife,
Sporting in that pleasing life,
That Coridon commendeth so,
All other liues to ouer-go.
He and she did sit and keepe
Flocks of kids, and fouldes of sheepe:
He vpon his pipe did play,
She tuned voice vnto his lay.
And for you might her Huswife knowe,
Voice did sing and fingers sowe:
He was young, his coat was greene,
With welts of white, seamde betweene,
Turned ouer with a flappe,
That brest and bosome in did wrappe,
Skirts side and plighted free,
Seemely hanging to his knee.
A whittle with a siluer chape,
Cloke was russet, and the cape
Serued for a Bonnet oft,
To shrowd him from the wet aloft.
A leather scrip of colour red,
With a button on the head,

A bottle full of Country whigge,
By the shepheards side did ligge:
And in a little bush hard by,
There the shepheards dogge did lye,
Who while his Master gan to sleepe,
Well could watch both kiddes and sheep.
The shepheard was a frolicke Swaine,
For though his parell was but plaine,
Yet doone the Authors soothly say,
His colour was both fresh and gay:
And in their writtes plaine discusse,
Fairer was not Tytirus,
Nor Menalcas whom they call
The Alderleefest swaine of all.
Seeming him was his wife,
Both in line, and in life:
Faire she was as faire might be,
Like the Roses on the tree:
Buxsane, blieth, and young, I weene
Beautious, like a sommers Queene,
For her cheekes were ruddy hued,
As if Lillies were imbrued,
With drops of bloud to make thee white,
Please the eye with more delight;
Loue did lye within her eyes,
In ambush for some wanton prize,
A leefer Lasse then this had beene,
Coridon had neuer seene.
Nor was Phillis that faire May,
Halfe so gawdy or so gay:
She wore a chaplet on her head,
Her cassocke was of scarlet red,
Long and large as streight as bent,
Her middle was both small and gent.
A necke as white as whales bone,
Compast with a lace of stone,
Fine she was and faire she was,
Brighter then the brightest glasse.
Such a Shepheards wife as she,
Was not more in Thessaly.

XLVIII

THE SHEPHEARDS WIVES SONG

Ah what is loue? It is a pretty thing,

As sweet vnto a shepheard as a king,
        And sweeter too:
For kings haue cares that waite vpon a Crowne,
And cares can make the sweetest loue to frowne:
        Ah then, ah then,
If countrie loues such sweet desires do gaine,
What Lady would not loue a Shepheard Swaine?

His flockes are foulded, he comes home at night,
As merry as a king in his delight,
        And merrier too:
For kings bethinke them what the state require,
Where Shepheards carelesse Carroll by the fire.
        Ah then, ah then,
If country loues such sweet desires gaine,
What Lady would not loue a Shepheard Swaine.
He kisseth first, then sits as blyth to eate

His creame and curds, as doth the king his meate;
        And blyther too:
For kings haue often feares when they do sup,
Where Shepheards dread no poyson in their cup.
        Ah then, ah then,
If country loues such sweet desires gaine,
What Lady would not loue a Shepheard Swaine.
To bed he goes, as wanton then I weene,
As is a king in dalliance with a Queene;
        More wanton too:
For kings haue many griefes affects to moue,
Where Shepheards haue no greater grief then loue:
        Ah then, ah then,
If countrie loues such sweet desires gaine,
What Lady would not loue a Shepheard Swaine.

Vpon his couch of straw he sleeps as sound,
As doth the king vpon his bed of downe,
        More sounder too:
For cares cause kings full oft their sleepe to spill,
Where weary Shepheards lye and snort their fill:
        Ah then, ah then,
If country loues such sweet desires gaine,
What Lady would not loue a Shepheard Swaine.

Thus with his wife he spends the yeare as blyth,
As doth the king at euery tyde or syth;
        And blyther too:
For kings haue warres and broyles to take in hand,
Where Shepheards laugh, and loue vpon the land.

Ah then, ah then,
If Countrie loues such sweet desires gaine,
What Lady would not loue a Shepheard Swaine?

XLIX

HEXAMETRA ALEXIS IN LAVDEM ROSAMVNDAE

Oft haue I heard my liefe Coridon report on a loue-day,
When bonny maides doe meete with the Swaines in the vally by Tempe,
How bright eyd his Phillis was, how louely they glanced,
When fro th' Aarches Eben black, flew lookes as a lightning,
That set a fire with piercing flames euen hearts adamantine,
Face Rose hued, Cherry red, with a siluer taint like a Lilly.
Venus pride might abate, might abash with a blush to behold her.
Phoebus wyers compar'd to her haires vnworthy the praysing.
Iunoes state, and Pallas wit disgrac'd with the Graces,
That grac'd her, whom poore Coridon did choose for a loue-mate:
Ah, but had Coridon now seene the starre that Alexis
Likes and loues so deare, that he melts to sighs when he sees her.
Did Coridon but see those eyes, those amorous eye-lids,
From whence fly holy flames of death or life in a moment,
Ah, did he see that face, those haires that Venus, Apollo
Basht to behold, and both disgrac'd, did grieue, that a creature
Should exceed in hue, compare both a god and a goddesse:
Ah, had he seene my sweet Paramour the Saint of Alexis,
Then had he sayd, Phillis, sit downe surpassed in all points,
For there is one more faire then thou, beloued of Alexis.

L

HEXAMETRA ROSAMVNDAE IN DOLOREM AMISSI ALEXIS

Tempe the groue where darke Hecate doth keep her abiding:
Tempe the groue where poor Rosamond bewails her Alexis,
Let not a tree nor a shrub be greene to shew thy reioycing;
Let not a leafe once decke thy boughes and branches, O Tempe,
Let not a bird record her tunes, nor chaunt any sweet Notes,
But Philomele, let her bewayle the losse of her amours,
And fill all the wood with dolefull tunes to bemone her,
Parched leaues fill euery Spring, fill euery Fountaine,
All the meades in mourning weede fit them to lamenting.
Eccho sit and sing despaire i' the Vallies, i' the Mountaines;
All Thessaly helpe poore Rosamond mournfull to bemone her:

For she's quite bereft of her loue, and left of Alexis,
Once was she lik'd, and once was she loued of wanton Alexis:
Now is she loathed, and now is she left of trothlesse Alexis.
Here did he clip and kisse Rosamond, and vowe by Diana:
None so deare to the Swaine as I, nor none so beloued,
Here did he deepely sweare, and call great Pan for a witnesse,
That Rosamond was onely the Rose belou'd of Alexis,
That Thessaly had not such an other Nymph to delight him:
None (quoth he) but Venus faire shall haue any kisses.
Not Phillis, were Phillis aliue should haue any fauours,
Nor Galate, Galate so faire for beautious eyebrowes,
Nor Doris that Lasse that drewe the Swaines to behold her:
Not one amongst all these, nor all should gaine any graces,
But Rosamond alone to her selfe should haue her Alexis.
Now to reuenge the periurde vowes of faithlesse Alexis,
Pan, great Pan, that heardst his othes, and mighty Diana,
You Dryades and watry Nymphs that sport by the Fountaines:
Fair Tempe the gladsome groue of greatest Apollo,
Shrubs, and dales, and neighbouring hils, that heard when he swore him,
Witnes all, and seeke to reuenge the wrongs of a Virgin,
Had any Swaine been liefe to me but guilefull Alexis,
Had Rosamond twinde Myrtle boughes, or Rosemary branches,
Sweet Holihocke, or else Daffadill, or slips of a Bay tree,
And giuen them for a gift to any Swaine but Alexis:
Well had Alexis done t' haue left his rose for a giglot.
But Galate nere lou'd more deare her louely Menalcas
Then Rosamond did dearely loue her trothlesse Alexis.
Endimion was nere beloued of his Citherea,
Halfe so deare as true Rosamond beloued her Alexis,
Now seely Lasse, hie downe to the lake, haste downe to the willowes,
And with those forsaken twigs go make thee a Chaplet,
Mournfull sit, and sigh by the springs, by the brookes, by the riuers,
Till thou turne for griefe, as did Niobe to a Marble,
Melt to teares, poure out thy plaints, let Eccho reclame them,
How Rosamond that loued so deare is left of Alexis,
Now dye, dye Rosamond, let men ingraue o' thy toombe-stone
Here lyes she that loued so deare the Youngster Alexis,
Once beloued, forsaken late of faithlesse Alexis:
Yet Rosamond did dye for loue false hearted Alexis.

LI

PHILADORS ODE THAT HE LEFT WITH THE DESPAIRING LOVER

When merry Autumne in her prime,
Fruitfull mother of swift time,

Had filled Ceres lappe with store
Of Vines and Corne, and mickle more,
Such needfull fruites as do growe
From Terras bosome here belowe,
Tytirus did sigh and see
With hearts griefe and eyes greee,
Eyes and heart both full of woes
Where Galate his louer goes,
Her mantle was vermillion red,
A gawdy Chaplet on her head,
A Chaplet that did shrowd the beames.
That Phoebus on her beauty streames
For Sunne it selfe desired to see
So faire a Nymph as was shee;
For, viewing from the East to West,
Faire Galate did like him best:
Her face was like to Welkins shine,
Crystall brookes such were his eyne:
And yet within those brookes were fires,
That scorched youth and his desires.
Galate did much impaire
Venus honour for her faire.
For stately stepping Iunoes pace,
By Galate did take disgrace:
And Pallas wisedome bare no prise,
Where Galate would shew her wise.
This gallant Girle thus passeth by
Where Tityrus did sighing lye:
Sighing sore for Loue straines
More then sighes from Louers vaines,
Teares in eye, thought in heart,
Thus his griefe he did impart.
Faire Galate but glance thine eye,
Here lyes he that here must dye:
For loue is death, if loue not gaine
Louers salue for Louers paine.
Winters seuen and more are past,
Since on thy face my thoughts I cast:
When Galate did haunt the Plaines,
And fed her sheepe amongst the Swaines:
When euery shepheard left his flockes,
To gaze on Galates faire lockes.
When euery eye did stand at gaze:
When heart and thought did both amaze,
When heart from body would asunder,
On Galates faire face to wonder:
Then amongst them all did I
Catch such a wound as I must dye

If Galate oft say not thus,
I loue the shepheard Tityrus.
Tis loue (faire nymph) that doth paine
Tytirus thy truest Swaine;
True, for none more true can be,
Then still to loue, and none but thee.
Say Galate, oft smile and say,
Twere pitty loue should haue a nay:
But such a word of comfort giue
And Tytirus thy Loue shall liue
Or with a piercing frowne reply
I cannot liue, and then I dye,
For Louers nay, is Louers death,
And heart breake frownes doth stop the breath.
Galate at this arose,
And with a smile away she goes,
As one that little carde to ease
Tytir, pain'd with Loues disease.
At her parting, Tytirus
Sighed amaine, and sayed thus:
Oh that women are so faire,
To trap mens eyes in their haire,
With beauteous eyes Loues fires,
Venus sparkes that heates desires:
But, oh that women haue such hearts,
Such thoughts, and such deep piercing darts,
As in the beauty of their eye,
Harbor nought but flattery:
Their teares are drawne that drop deceit,
Their faces, Calends of all sleight,
Their smiles are lures, their lookes guile,
And all their loue is but a wyle.
Then Tytir leaue leaue Tytirus
To loue such as scornes you thus:
And say to loue, and women both,
What I liked, now I do loath.
With that he hyed him to the flockes,
And counted loue but Venus mockes.

LII

THE SONG OF A COVNTRY SWAINE AT THE RETVRNE OF PHILADOR

The silent shade had shadowed euery tree,
And Phoebus in the west was shrowded low:
Ech hiue had home her busie laboring Bee,

Ech bird the harbour of the night did knowe,
  Euen then,
  When thus:
All things did from their weary labour linne,
Menalcas sate and thought him of his sinne.

His head on hand, his elbowe on his knee,
And teares, like dewe, be-drencht vpon his face,
His face as sad as any swaines might bee:
His thoughts and dumpes befitting wel the place.
  Euen then,
  When thus:
Menalcas sate in passions all alone,
He sighed then, and thus he gan to mone.

I that fed flockes vpon Thessalia plaines
And bad my lambs to feede on Daffadill,
That liued on milke and curdes poore Shepheards gaines
And merry sate, and pyp'd vpon a pleasant hill.
  Euen then,
  When thus:
I sate secure and fear'd not fortunes ire,
Mine eyes eclipst, fast blinded by desire.

Then lofty thoughts began to lift my minde,
I grudg'd and thought my fortune was too low,
A shepheards life 'twas base and out of kinde,
The tallest Cedars haue the fairest growe,
  Euen then,
  When thus:
Pride did intend the sequell of my ruth,
Began the faults and follies of my youth.

I left the fields, and tooke me to the Towne,
Fould sheepe who list, the hooke was cast away,
Menalcas would not be a country Clowne,
Nor Shepheards weeds, but garments far more gay.
  Euen then,
  When thus:
Aspiring thoughts did follow after ruth,
Began the faults and follies of my youth.

My sutes were silke, my talke was all of State,
I stretcht beyond the compasse of my sleeue,
The brauest Courtier was Menalcas mate,
Spend what I would, I neuer thought on griefe.
  Euen then,
  When thus:

I lasht out lauish, then began my ruth,
And then I felt the follies of my youth.

I cast mine eye on euery wanton face,
And straight desire did hale me on to loue,
Then Louer-like, I pray'd for Venus grace,
That she my mistris deepe affects might moue.
      Euen then,
      When thus:
Loue trapt me in the fatall bands of ruth,
Began the faults and follies of my youth.

No cost I spar'd to please my mistris eye,
No time ill spent in presence of her sight,
Yet oft she frownd, and then her loue must dye,
But when she smyl'd, oh then a happy wight.
      Euen then,
      When thus:
Desire did draw me on to deeme of ruth,
Began the faults and follies of my youth.

The day in poems often did I passe,
The night in sighs and sorrowes for her grace,
And she as fickle as the brittle glasse,
Held Sun-shine showres within her flattering face.
      Euen then,
      When thus:
I spy'd the woes that womens loues ensueth,
I saw, and loath the follies of my youth.

I noted oft that beauty was a blaze,
I saw that loue was but a heape of cares,
That such as stood as Deare do at the gaze,
And sought their welth amongst affections snares.
      Euen such,
      I sawe,
With hot pursuit did follow after ruth,
And fostered vp the follies of their youth.

Thus clogg'd with loue, with passions and with griefe,
I saw the country life had least molest,
I felt a wound and faine would haue reliefe,
And this resolu'd I thought would fall out best,
      Euen then,
      When thus:
I felt my senses almost solde to ruth,
I thought to leaue the follies of my youth,

To flockes againe, away the wanton towne,
Fond pride auaunt, giue me the shepheards hooke,
A coate of gray, He be a country clowne:
Mine eye shall scorne on beauty for to looke.
     No more,
     A doe:
Both Pride and loue are euer pain'd with ruth,
And therefore farewell the follies of my youth.

LIII

FROM NEVER TOO LATE

An Ode

Downe the valley gan he tracke,
Bagge and bottle at his backe,
In a surcoate all of gray,
Such weare Palmers on the way,
When with scrip and staffe they see
Iesus graue on Caluarie,
A hat of straw like a swaine,
Shealter for the sonne and raine,
With a Scollop shell before:
Sandalls on his feete he wore,
Legs were bare, armes vnclad,
Such attire this Palmer had,
His face faire like Titans shine,
Gray and buxsome were his eyne,
Whereout dropt pearles of sorrow:
Such sweete teares Loue doth borrow,
When in outward deawes he plaines,
Harts distresse that Louers paines:
Rubie lips, cherrie cheekes,
Such rare mixture Venus seekes,
When to keepe hir damsels quiet
Beautie sets them downe their diet.
Adon* was not thought more faire.
Curled lockes of amber haire:
Lockes where Loue did sit and twine
Nets to snare the gazers eyne:
Such a Palmer nere was seene,
Lesse loue himselfe had Palmer been.
Yet for all he was so quaint
Sorrow did his visage taint.
Midst the riches of his face,

Griefe decyphred hie disgrace:
Euerie step strain d a teare,
Sodaine sighes shewd his feare:
And yet his feare by his sight,
Ended in a strange delight.
That his passions did approue,
Weedes and sorrow were for loue.

LIV

The Palmers Ode

Olde Menalcas on a day,
As in field this shepheard lay,
Tuning of his oten pipe,
Which he hit with manie a stripe;
Said to Coridon that hee
Once was yong and full of glee,
Blithe and wanton was I then:
Such desires follow men.
As I lay and kept my sheepe,
Came the God that hateth sleepe,
Clad in armour all of fire,
Hand in hand with Queene Desire:
And with a dart that wounded nie,
Pearst my heart as I did lie:
That when I wooke I gan sweare,
Phillis beautie palme did beare.
Vp I start, foorth went I,
With hir face to feede mine eye:
Then I saw Desire sit,
That my heart with Loue had hit,
Laying foorth bright Beauties hookes.
To intrap my gazing lookes.
Loue I did and gan to woe;
Pray and sigh, all would not doe:
Women when they take the toy
Couet to be counted coy.
Coy she was, and I gan court,
She thought Loue was but a sport.
Profound Hell was in my thought,
Such a paine Desire had wrought,
That I sued with sighes and teares,
Still ingrate she stopt her eares,
Till my youth I had spent,
Last a passion of Repent,

Tolde me flat that Desire,
Was a brond of Loues fire,
Which consumeth men in thrall,
Vertue, youth, wit, and all.
At this sawe backe I start,
Bet Desire from my hart,
Shooke of Loue and made an oth,
To be enemie to both.
Olde I was when thus I fled,
Such fond toyes as cloyde my head.
But this I learn'd at Vertues gate,
The way to good is neuer late.
Nunquam sera est ad bonos mores via.

LV

THE HERMITES EXORDIVM

Here looke my sonne for no vaine glorious shewes.
Of royall apparition for the eye,
Humble and meeke befitteth men of yeeres,
Behold my cell built in a silent shade,
Holding content for pouertie and peace,
And in my lodge is fealtie and faith,
Labour and loue vnited in one league.
I want not, for my minde affordeth wealth;
I know not enuie, for I climbe not hie:
Thus do I Hue, and thus I meane to die.

If that the world presents illusions,
Or sathan seekes to pufle me vp with pompe,
As man is fraile and apt to follow pride:
Then see my sonne where I haue in my cell,
A dead mans scull, which cals this straight to mind,
That as this is, so must my ending be.
When then I see that earth to earth must passe,
I sigh, and say, all flesh is like to grasse.

If care to liue, or sweete delight in life,
As man desires to see out manie daies,
Drawes me to listen to the flattering world:
Then see my glasse which swiftly out doth runne,
Comparde to man, who dies ere he begins.
This tells me, time slackes not his poasting course,
But as the glasse runnes out with euerie hower,
Some in their youth, some in their weakest age,

All sure to die, but no man knowes his time.
By this I thinke, how vaine a thing is man,
Whose longest life is likened to a span.

When sathan seekes to sift me with his wiles,
Or proudly dares to giue a fierce assault,
To make a shipwracke of my faith with feares,
Then armde at all points to withstand the foe
With holy armour: heres the martiall sword:
This booke, this bible, this two-edged blade,
Whose sweete content pierceth the gates of hell:
Decyphring lawes and discipline of warre,
To ouerthrowe the strength of Sathans iarre.

LVI

ISABELLS ODE

Sitting by a riuer side,
Where a silent streame did glide,
Banckt about with choice of flowers,
Such as spring from Aprill showers,
When fair Iris smiling sheaws.
All her riches in her dewes,
Thicke leaued trees so were planted,
As nor arte nor nature wanted,
Bordring all the broke with shade,
As if Venus there had made
By Floraes wile a curious bowre,
To dally with her paramoure.
At this current as I gazd,
Eies intrapt, mind amazde,
I might see in my ken,
Such a flame as fireth men,
Such a fier as doth frie,
With one blaze both heart and eie,
Such a heate as dooth proue
No heate like to the heate of loue.
Bright she was, for twas a she,
That tracde hir steps towards me:
On her head she ware a bay,
To fence Phoebus light away:
In her face one might descrie
The curious beauty of the skie,
Her eies carried darts of fier,
Feathred all with swift desier,

Yet foorth these fierie darts did passe
Pearled teares as bright as glasse,
That wonder 'twas in her eine
Fire and water should combine:
If th' old sawe did not borrow,
Fier is loue, and water sorrow:
Downe she sate, pale and sad,
No mirth in her lookes she had,
Face and eies shewd distresse,
Inward sighes discourst no lesse:
Head on hand might I see,
Elbow leaned on hir knee,
Last she breathed out this saw,
Oh that loue hath no law.
Loue inforceth with constraint,
Loue delighteth in complaint;
Who so loues hates his life:
For loues peace is mindes strife.
Loue doth feede on beauties fare,
Euerie dish sawst with care:
Chiefly women, reason why,
Loue is hatcht in their eye:
Thence it steppeth to the hart,
There it poysneth euerie part:
Minde and heart, eye and thought,
Till sweete loue their woes hath wrought.
Then repentant they 'gin crie,
Oh my heart that trowed mine eye.
Thus she said and then she rose,
Face and minde both full of woes:
Flinging thence with this saw;
Fie on loue that hath no law.

LVII

FRANCESCOS ODE

When I looke about the place
Where sorrow nurseth vp disgrace,
Wrapt within a folde of cares,
Whose distresse no heart spares:
Eyes might looke, but see no light,
Heart might thinke but on despight,
Sonne did shine, but not on me:
Sorrow said it may not be,
That heart or eye should once possesse

Anie salue to cure distresse:
For men in prison must suppose
Their couches are the beds of woes.
Seeing this I sighed then,
Fortune thus should punish men.
But when I calde to minde her face
For whose loue I brooke this place,
Starrie eyes, whereat my sight,
Did eclipse with much delight,
Eyes that lighten and doo shine,
Beames of loue that are diuine,
Lilly cheekes whereon beside
Buds of Roses shew their pride,
Cherrie lips which did speake
Words that made all hearts to breake:
Words most sweete, for breath was sweete,
Such perfume for loue is meete.
Precious words, as hard to tell
Which more pleased, wit or smell
When I saw my greatest paines
Grow for hir that beautie staines.
Fortune thus I did reproue,
Nothing grieuefull growes from loue.

LVIII

CANZONE

As then the Sun sate lordly in his pride,
Not shadowed with the vale of any cloude:
The Welkin had no racke that seemd to glide,
No duskie vapour did bright Phoebus shroude:
  No blemish did eclipse the beauteous skie
  From setting foorth heauens secret searching eie,
No blustring winde did shake the shadie trees,
Each leafe lay still and silent in the wood,
The birds were musicall, the labouring Bees
That in the sommer heapes their winters good,
  Plied to the hiues sweet hony from those flowers,
  Whereout the serpent strengthens all his powers.
The lion laid and stretcht him in the lawnes,
No storme did hold the Leopard fro his pray,
The fallow fields were full of wanton fawnes,
The plough-swaines neuer saw a fairer day,
  For euery beast and bird did take delight
  To see the quiet heauens to shine so bright.

When thus the windes lay sleeping in the caues,
The ayre was silent in her concaue sphere,
And Neptune with a calme did please his slaues,
Ready to wash the neuer drenched Beare:
>Then did the change of my affects begin;
>And wanton loue assaid to snare me in.
Leaning my backe against a loftie pine,
Whose top did checke the pride of all the aire,
Fixing my thoughts, and with my thoughts mine eine
Vpon the Sunne, the fairest of all faire:
>What thing made God so faire as this, quoth I?
>And thus I musde vntill I darkt mine eie.
Finding the Sunne too glorious for my sight,
I glaunst my looke to shun so bright a lampe,
With that appeard an obiect twice as bright,
So gorgeous as my senses all were dampt.
>In Ida richer beautie did not win
>When louely Venus shewd her siluer skin.
Her pace was like to Iunoes pompous straines,
When as she sweeps through heuens brasse-paued way,
Her front was powdred through with azurde vaines,
That twixt sweet Roses and faire lillies lay,
>Reflecting such a mixture from her face,
>As tainted Venus beautie with disgrace,
>Arctophylax the brightest of the stars
>Was not so orient as her christall eies,
>Wherein triumphant sat both peace and wars,
>From out whose arches such sweete fauours flies,
>>As might reclaime Mars in his highest rage,
>>At beauties charge his fury to assuage.
The Diamond gleames not more reflecting lights,
Pointed with fiery pyramides to shine,
Than are those flames that burnish in our sights,
Darting fire out the christall of her eine,
>Able to set Narcissus thoughts on fier,
>Although he swore him foe to sweete desier.
Gazing vpon this lemman with mine eie,
I felt my sight vaile bonnet to her lookes,
So deepe a passion to my heart did flie,
As I was trapt within her luring hookes,
>Forst to confesse before that I had done,
>Her beauty farre more brighter than the Sunne.

LIX

INFIDAS SONG

Sweet Adon', darst not glaunce thine eye.
N'oserez vous, mon bel amy?
Vpon thy Venus that must die,
Ie vous en prie, pitie me:
N'oserez vous, mon bel, mon bel,
N'oserez vous, mon bel amy?
See how sad thy Venus lies,
N'oserez vous, mon bel amy?
Loue in heart and teares in eyes,
Je vous en prie, pitie me:
N'oserez vous, mon bel, mon bel,
N'oserez vous, mon bel amy?
Thy face as faire as Paphos brookes,
N'oserez vous, mon bel amy?
Wherein fancie baites her hookes,
Ie vous en prie, pitie me:
N'oserez vous, mon bel, mon bel,
N'oserez vous, mon bel amyl
Thy cheekes like cherries that doo growe,
N'oserez vous, mon bel amy?
Amongst the Westerne mounts of snowe,
Ie vous en prie, pitie me:
N'oserez vous, mon bel, mon bel,
N'oserez vous, mon bel amy?
Thy lips vermilion, full of loue,
N'oserez vous, mon bel amy?
Thy necke as siluer-white as doue,
Ie vous en prie, pitie me:
N'oserez vous, mon bel, mon bel
N'oserez vous, mon bel amy?
Thine eyes like flames of holie fires,
N'oserez vous, mon bel amy?
Burnes all my thoughts with sweete desires,
Ie vous en prie, pitie me:
N'oserez vous, mon bel, mon bel,
N'oserez vous, mon bel amy?
All thy beauties sting my hart,
Noserez vous, mon bel amy?
I must die through Cupid's dart,
Ie vous en prie, pitie me:
N'oserez vous, mon bel, mon bel,
N'oserez vous, bel amy?
Wilt thou let thy Venus die?
N'oserez vous, mon bel amy?
Adon were vnkinde, say I,
Ie vous en prie, pitie me:
N'oserez vous, mon bel, mon bel,

N'oserez vous, mon btl amy?
To let faire Venus die for woe,
N'oserez vous, mon bel amy?
That doth loue sweete Adon so;
Ie vous en prie, pitie me:
N'oserez vous, mon bel, mon bel,
JV'oserez vous, mon bel amy?

LX

FRANCESCOES ROVNDELAY

Sitting and sighing in my secret muse,
As once Apollo did, surprisde with loue,
Noting the slippery wayes young yeeres do vse,
What fond affects the prime of youth doth moue,
     With bitter teares despairing I do crie,
     'Wo worth the faults and follies of mine eie.'

When wanton age, the blossome of my time,
Drewe me to gaze vpon the gorgeous sight,
That beauty pompous in her highest prime,
Presents to tangle men with sweete delight,
     Then with despairing teares my thoughts did crie,
     'Wo worth the faults and follies of mine eie.'

When I surueid the riches of her lookes;
Whereout flew flames of neuer quencht desire,
Wherein lay baites, that Venus snares with hookes,
Oh, where proud Cupid sate all armde with fire:
     Then toucht with loue my inward soule did crie,
     'Wo worth the faultes and follies of mine eie.'

The milke white Galaxia of her brow,
Where Loue doth daunce lauoltas of his skill,
Like to the Temple, where true loners vow
To follow what shall please their Mistresse will,
     Noting her iuorie front, now do I crie,
     'Wo worth the faults and follies of mine eie.'

Hir face like siluer Luna in hir shine,
All tainted through with bright Vermillion straines,
Like lillies dipt in Bacchus choicest wine,
Powdred and interseamd with azurde vaines,
     Delighting in their pride now may I crie,
     'Wo worth the faults and follies of mine eie.'

The golden wyers that checkers in the day,
Inferiour to the tresses of her haire,
Her amber tramells did my heart dismay,
That when I lookte, I durst not ouer-dare:
   Prowd of her pride, now am I forst to cri,
    'Wo worth the faults and follies of mine eie.'

These fading beauties drew me on to sin,
Natures great riches framde my bitter ruth,
These were the trappes that loue did snare me in,
Oh, these, and none but these haue wrackt my youth.
   Misled by them, I may dispairing crie,
    'Wo worth the faults and follies of mine eie.'

By these I slipt from vertues holy tracke,
That leades vnto the highest Christall sphere,
By these I fell to vanitie and wracke,
And as a man forlorne with sin and feare,
   Despaire and sorrow doth constraine me crie,
    'Wo worth the faults and follies of mine eie.'

LXI

THE PENITENT PALMERS ODE

Whilome in the Winters rage
A Palmer old and full of age,
Sate and thought vpon his youth,
With eyes, teares, and harts ruth,
Being all with cares yblent,

When he thought on yeares mispent,
When his follies came to minde,
How fond loue had made him blinde,
And wrapt him in a field of woes,
Shadowed with pleasures shoes,
Then he sighed and said alas,
Man is sinne, and flesh is grasse.
I thought my mistris haires were gold,
And in her lockes my heart I folde:
Her amber tresses were the sight
That wrapped me in vaine delight:
Her luorie front, her pretie chin,
Were stales that drew me on to sin:
Her starrie lookes, her Christall eyes,

Brighter then the Sunnes arise:
Sparkling pleasing flames of fire,
Yoakt my thoughts and my desire,
That I gan crie ere I blin,
Oh her eyes are paths to sin.
Her face was faire, her breath was sweete,
All her lookes for loue was meete:
But loue is follie this I knowe,
And beautie fadeth like to snowe.
Oh why should man delight in pride,
Whose blossome like a deaw doth glide:
When these supposes toucht my thought,
That world was vaine, and beautie nought,
I gan sigh and say alas,
Man is sinne, and flesh is grasse.

LXII

ISABELS SONNET THAT SHE MADE IN PRISON

Veritas non quaerit Angulos

No storme so sharp to rent the little Reede,
For sild it breakes though euery way it bend,
The fire may heat but not consume the Flint,
The gold in furnace purer is indeede.
Report that sild to honour is a friend,
May many lies against true meaning mynt:
        But yet at last
        Gainst slaunders blast,
Truth doth the silly sackles soule defend.

Though false reproach seekes honour to distaine
And enuy bites the bud though nere so pure:
Though lust doth seek to blemish chast desire,
Yet truth that brookes not falshoods slaunderous staine,
Nor can the spight of enuies wrath indure,
Will trie true loue from lust in Iustice fire,
        And maulger all
        Will free from thrall
The guiltles soule that keepes his footing sure.

Where innocence triumpheth in her prime,
And guilt cannot approach the honest minde:
Where chast intent is free from any misse,
Though enuie striue, yet secret searching time,

With piercing insight will the truth out finde,
And make discouerie who the guiltie is:
>> For time still tries
>> The truth from lies,
And God makes open what the world doth blinde.

Veritas temporis filia.

FRANCESCOS SONNET, MADE IN THE PRIME OF HIS PENAVNCE

With sweating browes I long haue plowde the sandes:
My seede was youth, my croppe was endlesse care:
Repent hath sent me home with emptie hands
At last, to tell how rife our follies are:
>> And time hath left experience to approue:
>> The gaine is griefe to those that traffique loue.
The silent thoughts of my repentant yeeres
That fill my head, haue cald me home at last:
Now loue vnmaskt a wanton wretch apeares;
Begot by guilefull thought with ouer hast,
>> In prime of youth a rose, in age a weede,
>> That for a minutes ioye payes endlesse neede.
Dead to delights, a foe to fond conceipt,
Allied to wit by want, and sorrow bought:
Farewell fond youth, long fostred in deceipt:
Forgiue me Time disguisd idle thought.
>> And Loue adew, loe hasting to mine ende;
>> I finde no time too late for to amend.

LXIV

FRANCESCOS SONNET CALD HIS PARTING BLOW

Reason that long in prison of my will
Hast wept thy mistris wants and losse of time:
Thy wonted siege of honour safely clime,
To thee I yeeld as guiltie of mine ill.

Lo (fettered in their teares) mine eyes are prest
To pay due homage to their natiue guide,
My wretched heart wounded with bad betide,
To craue his peace from reason, is addrest.

My thoughts ashamd since by themselues consumd
Haue done their duetie to repentant wit:
Ashamde of all sweete guide I sorie sit,
To see in youth how I too farre presumde,

That he whom loue and errour did betray,
Subscribes to thee, and takes the better way.

Sero sed serio.

LXV

EVRYMACHVS FANCIE IN THE PRIME OF HIS AFFECTION

When lordly Saturne in a sable roabe
Sat full of frownes and mourning in the West,
The euening starre scarce peept from out her lodge
And Phoebus newly gallopt to his rest:
                    Euen then
                    Did I
Within my boate sit in the silent streames,
And voyd of cares as he that lies and dreames.

As Phao so a Ferriman I was,
The countrie lasses sayd I was too faire,
With easie toyle I labourd at mine oare,
To passe from side to side who did repaire:
                    And then
                    Did I
For paines take pence, and Charon like transport
Assoone the swayne as men of high import.

When want of worke did giue me leaue to rest,
My sport was catching of the wanton fish:
So did I weare the tedious time away,
And with my labour mended oft my dish:
                    For why
                    I thought
That idle houres were Calenders of ruth
And time ill spent was preiudice to youth.

I scornd to loue, for were the Nimph as faire,
As she that loued the beauteous Latmian swayne,
Her face, her eyes, her tresses, nor her browes
Like Iuorie could my affection gaine:

For why
I said
With high disdaine, Loue is a base desire,
And Cupids flames, why the'are but watrie fire.

As thus I sat disdayning of proud loue,
Haue ouer Ferriman there cried a boy,
And with him was a paragon, for hue
A louely damosell beauteous and coy,
                    And there
                    With her
A maiden, couered with a tawnie vale,
Her face vnseene for breeding louers bale.

I stird my boate, and when I came to shoare
The boy was wingd, me thought it was a wonder:
The dame had eyes like lightning, or the flash
That runnes before the hot report of thunder:
                    Her smiles
                    Were sweete,
Louely her face: was neere so faire a creature,
For earthly carkasse had a heauenly feature.

My friend (quoth she) sweete Ferriman behold,
We three must passe, but not a farthing fare,
But I will giue (for I am Queene of loue)
The brightest lasse thou lik'st vnto thy share,
                    Choose where
                    Thou louest
Be she as faire as Loues sweet Ladie is,
She shall be thine if that will be thy blisse.

With that she smiled with such a pleasing face,
As might haue made the marble rocke relent:
But I that triumpht in disdaine of loue,
Bad fie on him that to fond loue was bent,
                    And then
                    Said thus,
So light the Ferriman for loue doth care,
As Venus passe not, if she pay no fare.

At this a frowne sat on her angrie brow,
She winkes vpon her wanton sonne hard by:
He from his quiuer drew a bolt of fire,
And aymd so right as that he pearst mine eye:
                    And then
                    Did she
Draw downe the vale that hid the virgins face,

Whose heauenly beautie lightned all the place,
Straight then I leande mine eare vpon mine arme,
And lookt vpon the Nymph (if so) was faire:
Her eyes were starres, and like Apollos locks,
The thought appeard the tramels of her haire,
                    Thus did
                    I gaze
And suckt in beautie till that sweete desire
Cast fuell on and set my thought on fire.

When I was lodgd within the net of loue
And that they saw my heart was all on flame,
The Nymph away, and with her trips along
The winged boy, and with her goes his dame.
                    Oh then
                    I cried
Stay Ladies stay and take not any care,
You all shall passe and pay no penny fare.

Away they fling, and looking coylie backe
They laugh at me: oh with a loude disdaine
I send out sighes to ouertake the Nimph,
And teares as lures to call them backe againe:
                    But they
                    Flie thence,
But I sit in my boate, with hand on oare,
And feele a paine, but knowe not whats the sore.

At last I feele it is the flame of loue,
I striue but bootlesse to expresse the paine,
It cooles, it fires, it hopes, it feares, it frets,
And stirreth passions throughout euery vaine.
                    That downe
                    I sat,
And sighing did faire Venus lawes approoue,
And swore no thing so sweete and sowre as loue.

Et florida pungunt.

LXVI

RADAGONS SONNET

No cleare appeard vpon the azurd Skie,
A vale of stormes had shaddowed Phoebus face,
And in a sable mantle of disgrace,

Sate he that is ycleaptd heauens bright eye,
    As though that he,

Perplext for Clitia, meant to leaue his place,
And wrapt in sorrowes did resolue to die:
For death to louers woes is euer nie:
Thus foulded in a hard and mournfull laze
    Distrest sate hee.

A mistie fogge had thickened all the ayre,
Iris sate solemne and denied her showers:
Flora in taunie hid vp all her flowers
And would not diaper her meads with faire,
    As though that shee

Were armd vpon the barren earth to lowre.
Vnto the founts Diana nild repaire,
But sate as ouershadowed with despaire,
Solemne and sad within a withered bower
    Her Nymphes and she.

Mars malecontent lay sick on Venus knee,
Venus in dumps sat muffled with a frowne,
Iuno laid all her frollick humors downe,
And Ioue was all in dumps as well as she:
    Twas Fates decree.

For Neptune (as he ment the world to drown)
Heaud vp his surges to the highest tree,
And leagud with Eol, mard the Seamans glee,
Beating the Cedars with his billows downe,
    Thus wroth was hee.

My mistris deynes to shew hir sunbright face,
The ayre cleard vp, the clowds did fade away,
Phoebus was frollick when she did display,
The gorgious bewties, that her frunt do grace,
    So that when shee

But walkt abroad, the stormes then fled away.
Flora did checker all her treading place,
And Neptune calmde the surges with his mace,
Diana and hir Nimphes were blithe and gaie,
    When her they see.

Venus and Mars agreed in a smile:
And iealous Iuno ceased now to lowre,
Ioue saw her face and sighed in his bowre:

Iris and Eol laugh within a while
    To see this glee:

Ah borne was she within a happy howre
That makes heauen, earth, and gods and all to smile,
Such wonders can her beauteous lookes compile,
To cleare the world from any froward lowre,
    Ah blest be shee.

LXVII

EVRIMACHVS IN LAVDEM MIRIMIDÆ HIS MOTTO

Inuita fortuna dedi vota concordia.

When Flora proude in pompe of all her flowers
    Sat bright and gay,
And gloried in the deaw of Iris showers,
    And did display
Her mantle checquered all with gawdy greene:
    Then I
    Alone
A mournfull man in Erecine was seene.

With folded armes I trampled through the grasse,
    Tracing as he
That held the Throane of Fortune brittle glasse,
    And loue to be
Like Fortune fleeting, as the restlesse wind
    Mixed
    With mists
Whose dampe doth make the cleerest eyes grow blind.

Thus in a maze I spied a hideous flame,
    I cast my sight,
And sawe where blythly bathing in the same
    With great delight,
A worme did lye, wrapt in a smokie sweate:
    And yet
    Twas strange
It carelesse lay and shrunke not at the heate.

I stood amazd and wondring at the sight,
    While that a dame
That shone like to the heauens rich sparkling light,
    Discourst the same:

And sayd, my friend this worme within the fire
Which lies
Content,
Is Venus worme, and represents desire.

A Salamander is this princely beast,
Deckt with a crowne,
Giuen him by Cupid as a gorgeous crest
Gainst fortunes frowne,
Content he lies and bathes him in the flame,
And goes
Not foorth:
For why he cannot liue without the same.

As he: so louers lie within the fire
Of feruent loue,
And shrinke not from the flame of hot desire,
Nor will not mooue
From any heate, that Venus force imparts:
But lie
Content
Within a fire and wast away their harts.

Vp flew the dame and vanisht in a clowde,
But there stood I,
And many thoughts within my mind did shrowd
My loue: for why,
I felt within my heart a scortching fire,
And yet
As did
The Salamander, twas my whole desire.

LXVIII

RADAGON IN DIANAM

Non fuga Teucrus amat: quae tamen odit habet.
It was a valley gawdie greene,
Where Dian at the fount was seene,
Greene it was,
And did passe
All other of Dianas bowers,
In the pride of Floras flowers.

A fount it was that no Sunne sees,
Circled in with Cipres trees,

Set so nie,
As Phoebus eye
Could not doo the Virgins scathe,
To see them naked when they bathe.

She sat there all in white,
Colour fitting her delite,
Virgins so
Ought to go:
For white in Armorie is plast
To be the colour that is chast.

Her tafta Cassocke might you see,
Tucked vp aboue her knee,
Which did show
There below
Legges as white as whales bone.
So white and chast was neuer none.

Hard by her vpon the ground,
Sat her Virgins in a round
Bathing their
Golden haire,
And singing all in notes hye
Fie on Venus flattring eye.

Fie on loue it is a toy,
Cupid witlesse and a boy,
All her fires
And desires
Are plagues that God sent downe from hie,
To pester men with miserie.

As thus the Virgins did disdaine,
Louers ioy and Louers paine,
Cupid nie
Did espie,
Greeuing at Dianas song,
Slylie stole these maides among.

His bow of steele, darts of fire,
He shot amongst them sweete desire,
Which straight flies
In their eyes,
And at the entrance made them start,
For it ran from eye to hart.

Calisto straight supposed loue

Was faire and frolicke for to loue:
Dian shee
Scapt not free:
For well I wot hereupon
She loued the swayne Endimion.

Clitia, Phoebus, and Cloris eye
Thought none so faire as Mercurie:
Venus thus
Did discusse
By her sonne in darts of fire,
None so chast to checke desire.

Dian rose with all her maids,
Blushing thus at loues braids,
With sighs all
Shew their thrall,
And flinging hence pronounce this saw,
What so strong as Loues sweet law?

LXIX

MVLLIDORS MADRIGALE

Dildido dildido,
Oh loue, oh loue,
I feele thy rage romble below and aboue.
In sommer time I sawe a face,
Trop belle pour moy hilas helas,
Like to a stoand horse was her pace:
Was euer yong man so dismaid,
Her eyes like waxe torches did make me afraid,
Trop belle pour moy, voila mon trespas.
Thy beautie (my Loue) exceedeth supposes,
Thy haire is a nettle for the nicest roses,
Mon dieu, aide moy,
That I with the primrose of my fresh wit,
May tumble her tyrannie vnder my feete,
HI donque ie sera un ieune roy.
Trop belle pour moy, helas helas,
Trop belle pour moy y voyla mon trespas.

LXX

In greener yeares when as my greedie thoughts
Gan yeeld their homage to ambitions will,
My feeble wit that then preuailed noughts,
Perforce presented homage to his ill:
>And I in follies bondes fulfild with crime,
>At last vnloosd: thus spide my losse of time.

As in his circuler and ceaselesse ray
The yeare begins, and in it selfe returnes
Refresht by presence of the eye of day,
That sometimes nie and sometimes farre soiournes,
So loue in me (conspiring my decay)
With endles fire my heedles bosome burnes,
>And from the end of my aspiring sinne,
>My paths of error hourely doth begin.

Aries
When in the Ram the Sunne renewes his beames,
Beholding mournfull earth araid in griefe,
That waights reliefe from his refreshing gleames,
The tender flockes reioycing their reliefe,
Doe leape for ioy and lap the siluer streames,
So at my prime when youth in me was chiefe,
>All Heifer like with wanton home I playd,
>And by my will my wit to loue betrayd.

Taurus
When Phoebus with Europa's bearer bides,
The Spring appeares, impatient of delaies,
The labourer to the fields his plow-swaynes guides,
He sowes, he plants, he builds at all assaies,
When prime of yeares that many errors hides,
By fancies force did trace vngodiy waies,
>I blindfold walkt, disdayning to behold,
>That life doth vade, and yong men must be old.

Gemini
When in the hold whereas the Twins doo rest,
Proud Phlaegon breathing fire doth last amaine:
The trees with leaues, the earth with flowers is drest,
When I in pride of yeres with peeuish braine
Presum'd too farre and made fond loue my guest;
With frosts of care my flowers were nipt amaine.
>In height of weale who beares a careles hart,
>Repents too late his ouer foolish part.

Cancer

When in Aestiuall Cancers gloomie bower,
The greater glorie of the heauens dooth shine;
The aire is calme, the birds at euerie stowre
Do tempt the heauens with harmonie diuine,
When I was first inthrald to Cupids powre,
In vaine I spent the May-month of my time,
      Singing for joy to see me captiue thrall
      To him, whose gaines are greefe, whose comfort smal.

Leo

When in the height of his Miridian walke,
The Lions holde conteines the eye of day,
The riping come growes yeolow in the stalke,
When strength of yeares did blesse me euerie way.
Maskt with delights of follie was my talke,
Youth ripened all my thoughts to my decay:
      In lust I sowde, my frute was losse of time;
      My hopes were proud, and yet my bodie slime.

Virgo

When in the Virgins lap earths comfort sleepes,
Bating the furie of his burning eyes,
Both corne and frutes are firmd and comfort creepes
On euerie plant and flowre that springing rise:
When age at last his chiefe dominion keepes,
And leades me on to see my vanities;
      What loue and scant foresight did make me sowe
      In youthfull yeares, is ripened now in woe.

Libra

When in the Ballance Daphnes Lemman blins
The Ploughman gathereth frute for passed paine
When I at last considered of my sinnes,
And thought vpon my youth and follies vaine,
I cast my count, and reason now begins
To guide mine eyes with iudgement, bought with paine,
      Which weeping wish a better way to finde,
      Or els for euer to the world be blinde.

Scorpio

When with the Scorpion proud Apollo plaies,
The wines are trode and carried to their presse,
The woods are feld gainst winters sharpe affraies:
When grauer yeares my iudgements did addresse,
I gan repaire my ruines and decaies:
Exchanging will to wit and soothfastnesse:
      Claiming from Time and Age no good but this,

To see my sinne, and sorrow for my misse.

Sagittarius
When as the Archer in his Winter holde
The Delian Harper tunes his wonted loue,
The ploughman sowes and tills his labored molde;
When with aduise and iudgement I approue,
How Loue in youth hath griefe for gladnes solde,
The seedes of shame I from my heart remooue,
      And in their steads I set downe plants of grace,
      And with repent bewaile my youthfull race.

Capricornus
When he that in Eurotas siluer glide
Doth baine his tresse, beholdeth Capricorne,
The daies growes short, then hasts the winters tide,
The Sun with sparing lights doth seeme to mourn,
Gray is the green, the flowers their beautie hides:
When as I see that I to death was borne,
      My strength decaide, my graue alreadie drest,
      I count my life my losse, my death my best.

Aquarius
When with Aquarius Phoebes brother staies,
The blythe and wanton windes are whist and still,
Cold frost and snow the pride of earth betraies:
When age my head with hoarie haires doth fill,
Reason sits downe, and bids mee count my dayes,
And pray for peace, and blame my froward will:
      In depth of griefe in this distresse I crie,
      Peccaui Domine, miserere mei.

Pisces
When in the Fishes mansion Phoebus dwells,
The dayes renew, the earth regaines his rest:
When olde in yeares, my want my death foretells:
My thoghts and praiers to heauen are whole addrest,
Repentance youthly follie quite expells,
I long to be dissolued for my best,
      That yong in zeale long beaten with my rod,
      I may grow old to wisedome and to God. no

DESCRIPTION OF THE LADIE MAESIA

Hir stature and hir shape was passing tall,
Diana like, when longst the lawnes she goes,
A stately pace like Iuno when she braued,
The queene of heauen fore Paris in the vale,
A front beset with loue and maiestie,
A face like louely Venus when she blusht
A seely shepherd shoulde be beauties iudge,
A lip sweete rubie red, gracd with delight,
Hir eies two sparkling starres in winter night,
When chilling frost doth cleere the azurd skie,
Hir haires in tresses twind with threds of silke,
Hoong wauing downe like Phoebus in his prime:
Hir breasts as white as those two snowie swannes
That drawes to Paphos Cupids smiling dame:
A foote like Thetis when she tript the sands,
To steale Neptunus fauour with his steps:
In line, a peece despight of beauty framd,
To see what natures cunning could affoord.

LXXII

MAESIA'S SONG

Sweet are the thoughts that sauour of content,
        the quiet mind is richer than a crowne,
Sweet are the nights in carelesse slumber spent,
        the poore estate scornes fortunes angrie frowne.
Such sweet content, such minds, such sleep, such blis
        beggers inioy, when Princes oft do mis.

The homely house that harbors quiet rest,
        the cottage that affoords no pride nor care,
The meane that grees with Countrie musick best,
        the sweet consort of mirth and musicks fare,
Obscured life sets downe a type of blis,
        a minde content both crowne and kingdome is.

LXXIII

LINES TRANSLATED FROM GVAZZO

He that appaled with lust would saile in hast to Corinthum,
There to be taught in Layis schoole to seeke for a mistresse,
Is to be traind in Venus troupe and changd to the purpose,

Rage imbraced but reason quite thrust out as on exile,
Pleasure a paine rest tournd to be care and mirth as a madnesse,
Firie mindes inflamd with a looke imaged as Alecto,
Quaint in aray, sighs fetcht from farre, and teares many fained,
Pen sicke sore depe plungd in paine, not a place but his hart whole,
Daies in griefe and nights consumed to thinke on a goddesse,
Broken sleeps, swete dreams but short fro the night to the morning
Venus dasht his mistresse face as bright as Apollo,
Helena staind the golden ball wrong giuen by the sheepheard,
Haires of gold eyes twinckling starres hir lips to be rubies,
Teeth of pearle hir brests like snow hir cheekes to be roses.
Sugar candie she is as I gesse fro the wast to the kneestead.
Nought is amisse no fault were found if soule were amended.
All were blisse if such fond lust led not to repentance.

LXXIV

FROM DANTE

A monster seated in the midst of men,
Which daily fed is neuer satiat,
A hollow gulfe of vild ingratitude,
Which for his food vouchsafes not pay of thankes,
But still doth claime a debt of due expence,
From hence doth Venus draw the shape of lust,
From hence Mars raiseth bloud and stratagemes,
The wracke of wealth the secret foe to life,
The sword that hastneth on the date of death,
The surest friend to phisicke by disease,
The pumice that defaceth memorie,
The misty vapour that obscures the light,
And brightest beames of science glittring sunne,
And doth eclipse the minde with sluggish thoughtes,
The monster that afoordes this cursed brood,
And makes commixture of these dyer mishaps,
Is but a stomach ouerchargd with meates,
That takes delight in endlesse gluttony.

LXXV

PHILOMELAS ODE THAT SHEE SVNG IN HER ARBOVR

Sitting by a Riuers side,
Where a silent streame did glide,

Muse I did of many things,
That the mind in quiet brings.
I gan thinke how some men deeme
Gold their god, and some esteeme
Honour is the chiefe content,
That to man in life is lent.
And some others doe contend,
Quiet none, like to a friend.
Others hold, there is no wealth
Compared to a perfect health.
Some mans mind in quiet stands,
When he is Lord of many lands.
But I did sigh, and sayd all this
Was but a shade of perfect blis.
And in my thoughts I did approue,
Nought so sweet as is true loue,
Loue twixt louers passeth these,
When mouth kisseth and hart grees,
With folded armes and lippes meeting,
Each soule another sweetly greeting.
For by the breath the soule fleeteth,
And soule with soule in kissing meeteth.
If Loue be so sweet a thing,
That such happy blisse doth bring,
Happy is loues sugred thrall,
But vnhappy maydens all,
Who esteeme your Virgins blisses,
Sweeter then a wiues sweet kisses.
No such quiet to the mind,
As true loue with kisses kind.
But if a kisse proue vnchast,
Then is true loue quite disgrast.
Though loue be sweet, learn this of me
No loue sweet but honesty.

LXXVI

PHILOMELAES SECOND OADE

It was frosty winter season,
Meades that earst with greene were spred,
With choyce flowers diapred,
Had tawny vales: cold had scanted
What the Spring and Nature planted:
Leauelesse boughes there might you see,
All except fayre Daphnes tree,

On their twigs no byrdes pearched,
Warmer couerts now they searched;
And by Natures secret reason,
Trained their voyces to the season:
With their feeble tunes bewraying,
How they grieued the springs decaying:
Frosty Winter thus had gloomed
Each fayre thing that sommer bloomed,
Fields were bare, and trees vnclad,
Flowers withered, byrdes were sad:
When I saw a shepheard fold,
Sheepe in Coate to shunne the cold:
Himselfe sitting on the grasse,
That with frost withered was:
Sighing deepely, thus gan say,
Loue is folly when astray:
Like to loue no passion such,
For 'tis madnesse, if too much:
If too little, then despaire:
If too high, he beates the ayre;
With bootlesse cries, if too low:
An eagle matcheth with a crow.
Thence growes iarres, thus I find,
Loue is folly, if vnkind;
Yet doe men most desire
To be heated with this fire:
Whose flame is so pleasing hot,
That they burne, yet feele it not:
Yet hath loue another kind,
Worse than these vnto the mind:
That is, when a wantons eye
Leades desire cleane awry,
And with the Bee doth reioyce,
Euery minute to change choyce,
Counting he were then in blisse,
If that each fare fere were his:
Highly thus is loue disgraste,
When the louer is vnchaste;
And would taste of fruit forbidden,
Cause the scape is easily hidden.
Though such loue be sweet in brewing
Bitter is the end ensuing;
For the honour of loue he shameth,
And himselfe with lust defameth;
For a minutes pleasure gayning,
Fame and honour euer stayning,
Gazing thus so farre awry,
Last the chip fals in his eye,

Then it burns that earst but heate him,
And his owne rod gins to beate him;
His choycest sweets turne to gall,
He finds lust his sins thrall:
That wanton women in their eyes,
Mens deceiuings doe comprise.
That homage done to fayre faces,
Doth dishonour other graces:
If lawlesse loue be such a sinne,
Curst is he that hues therein:
For the gaine of Venus game,
Is the downefalle vnto shame:
Here he paus'd and did stay,
Sigh'd and rose, and went away.

LXXVII

LVLESIO'S SONNET

Naiura nihil frustra

On women Nature did bestow two eyes,
Like Heauen's bright lamps, in matchles beauty shining,
Whose beames doe soonest captiuate the wise
And wary heads, made rare by arts refining.
But why did Nature in her choyce combining,
Plant two faire eyes within a beautious face,
That they might fauour two with equall grace?

Venus did sooth vp Vulcan with one eye,
With th' other granted Mars his wished glee:
If she did so, who Hymen did defie,
Thinke loue no sinne, but grant an eye to me,
In vayne else Nature gaue two stars to thee:
If then two eyes may well two friends maintaine,
Allow of two, and proue not Nature vayne.

Natura repugnare belluinum.

LXXVIII

POEME IN ANSWER

Quot Cor da, tot Amores

Nature foreseeing how men would deuise
More wiles than Protheus, women to entise,
Graunted them two, and those bright shining eyes,
To pearce into men's faults if they were wise.
For they with shew of vertue maske their vice,
Therefore to women's eyes belongs these gifts,
The one must loue, the other see mens shifts.

Both these await vpon one simple heart,
And what they choose, it hides vp without change.
The Emrauld will not with his portraite part,
Nor will a womans thoughts delight to range.
They hold it bad to haue so base exchange.
One heart, one friend, though that two eyes do choose him,
No more but one, and heart will neuer loose him.

Cor unum, Amor unus.

LXXIX

AN ODE

What is loue once disgraced?
But a wanton thought ill placed,
Which doth blemish whom it payneth,
And dishonours whom it daineth,
Seene in higher powers most,
Though some fooles doe fondly bost,
That who so is high of kin,
Sanctifies his louers sinne.
Ioue could not hide Ios scape,
Nor conceale Calistos rape.
Both did fault, and both were framed,
Light of loues, whom lust had shamed.
Let not women trust to men,
They can flatter now and then.
And tell them many wanton tales,
Which doe breed their after bales.
Sinne in kings, is sinne wee see,
And greater sinne, cause great of gree.
Mains peccatum, this I reed,
If he be high that doth the deed.
Mars for all his Deity,
Could not Venus dignifie,
But Vulcan trapt her, and her blame

Was punisht with an open shame.
All the gods laught them to scorne,
For dubbing Vulcan with the home.
Whereon may a woman bost,
If her chastity be lost.
Shame awaitt'h vpon her face,
Blushing cheekes and foule disgrace,
Report will blab, this is she
That with her lust wins infamy,
If lusting loue be so disgrac't,
Die before you liue vnchast:
For better die with honest fame,
Then lead a wanton life with shame.

LXXX

FAMILIAS SONG

> Fie, fie on blind fancie,
> It hinders youths ioy:
> Fayre Virgins learne by me,
> To count loue a toy.

When Loue learned first the A. B. C. of delight,
And knew no figures, nor conceited Phrase:
He simplie gaue to due desert her right,
He led not Louers in darke winding wayes,
He plainly wild to loue, or flatly answered no,
But now who lists to proue, shall find it nothing so.

> Fie, fie then on fancie,
> It hinders youths ioy,
> Fayre Virgins learne by me,
> To count loue a toy.

For since he learnd to vse the Poets pen,
He learnde likewise with smoothing words to faine,
Witching chast eares with trothlesse toungs of men,
And wronged faith with falshood and disdaine.
He giues a promise now, anon he sweareth no,
Who listeth for to proue, shall finde his changing so:

> Fie, fie then on fancie,
> It hinders youthes joy,
> Fayre Virgins learne by me,
> To count loue a toy.

LXXXI

AGAINST ENTICING CVRTIZANS

What meant the Poets in inuectiue verse,
To sing Medeas shame, and Scillas pride,
Calipsoes charmes, by which so many dide?
Onely for this, their vices they rehearse,
That curious wits which in this world conuerse
May shun the dangers and entising shoes
Of such false Syrens, those home breeding foes
That from their eyes their venim do disperse.
So soone kils not the Basiliske with sight,
The Vipers tooth is not so venomous,
The Adders toung not halfe so daungerous,
As they that beare the shadow of delight,
Who chain blind youths in tramels of their hayre,
Till wast bring woe, and sorrow hasts despayre.

LXXXII

VERSES

Deceyuing world that with alluring toyes,
Hast made my life the subiect of thy scome:
And scornest now to lend thy fading ioyes,
To lengthen my life, whom friends haue left forlorn
How well are they that die ere they be borne.
      And neuer see thy sleights, which few men shun
      Till vnawares they helpelesse are vndone.

Oft haue I sung of loue and of his fire,
But now I finde that Poet was advizde
Which made full feasts increasers of desire,
And proues weak loue was with the poor despizde:
For when the life with food is not suffizde,
      What thoughts of loue, what motion of delight,
      What pleasance can proceed from such a wight?

Witnes my want the murderer of my wit,
My rauisht sense of woonted fury reft,
Wants such conceit, as should in Poems fit,
Set downe the sorrow wherein I am left,
But therefore haue high heauens, their gifts bereft.
      Because so long they lent them me to vse,
      And I so long their bounty did abuse.

O that a yeere were graunted me to liue,
And for that yeare my former wits restorde,
What rules of life, what counsell would I giue?
How should my sinne with sorrow be deplorde?
But I must die of euery man abhorde,
      Time loosely spent will not againe be woone,
      My time is loosely spent, and I vndone.

LXXXIII

A CONCEITED FABLE OF THE OLDE COMEDIAN AESOP

An Ant and a Grashopper walking together on a greene, the one carelessly skiping, the other carefully prying what Winters prouision was scattered in the way: the Grashopper scorning (as wantons will) this needelesse thrift (as he tearmed it) reprooued him thus.

The greedie miser thirsteth still for gaine,
His thrift is theft, his weale workes others woe,
That foole is fond which will in caues remaine,
When mongst faire sweetes he may at pleasure goe.

To this the Ant perceyuing the Grashoppers meaning, quickly replyed:

The thriftie husband spares what vnthrifts spends
His thrift no theft, for dangers to prouide;
Trust to thy selfe, small hope in want yeeld friends
A caue is better then the desarts wide.

In short time these two parted, the one to his pleasure, the other to his labor. Anon Harvest grew on, and reft from the Grashopper his wonted moysture. Then weakely skippes he to the medows brinks, where till fell winter he abode. But storms continually powring, he went for succour to the Ant his olde acquaintance, to whom he had scarce discouered his estate, but the little worme made this replie.

Packe hence (quoth he) thou idle lazie worme,
My house doth harbour no vnthriftie mates:
Thou scornedst to toyle, and now thou feelst the storm
And starvst for food, while I am fed with cates,
      Vse no intreats, I will relentlesse rest,
      For toyling labour hates an idle guest.

The Grashopper foodies, helpelesse, and strengthlesse, got into the next brooke and in the yeelding sand digde himselfe a pitte: by which likewise he ingraued this Epitaph:

When Springs greene prime arrayde me with delight,
And euery power with youthfull vigour fild,
Gaue strength to worke what euer fancie wild,

I neuer fearde the force of winters spight.
When first I saw the Sunne, the day beginne,
And drie the mornings teares from hearbes and grasse,
I little thought his chearefull light would passe,
Till vgly night with darkenesse enterd in,
     And then day lost I mournde, spring past I waild,
     But neither teares for this or that auaild,

Then too too late I praisde the Emmets paine,
That sought in spring a harbour gainst the heate,
And in the haruest gathered winters meate,
Perceiuing famine, frosts, and stormie raine.

My wretched end may warne Greene springing youth,
To vse delights, as toyes that will deceiue,
And scorne the world, before the world them leaue,
For all worlds trust, is ruine without ruth.
     Then blest are they that like the toyling Ant,
     Prouide in time gainst winters wofull want.

With this the Grashopper yeelding to the weathers extremitie, died comfortlesse without remedie. Like him my selfe: like me, shall all that trust to friends or times inconstancie. Now faint I of my last infirmitie, beseeching them that shall burie my bodie, to publish this last farewell, written with my wretched hand.

Faelicem fuisse infaustum.

LXXXIV

GREENES ODE, OF THE VANITIE OF WANTON WRITINGS

Though Tytirus the Heards Swaine,
Phillis loue-mate felt the paine,
That Cupid fiers in the eie,
Till they loue or till they die,
Straigned ditties from his pipe,
With pleasant voyce and cunning stripe:
Telling in his song how faire,
Phillis eie-browes and hir haire.
How hir face past all supposes:
For white Lillies: for red Roses.
Though he sounded on the hils,
Such fond passions as loue wils,
That all the Swaines that foulded by,
Flockt to heare his harmonie,
And vowed by Pan that Tytirus

Did Poet-like his loues discusse,
That men might learne mickle good,
By the verdict of his mood,
Yet olde Menalcas ouer-ag'd,
That many winters there had wag'd,
Sitting by and hearing this:
Said, their wordes were all amisse.
For (quoth he) such wanton laies,
Are not worthie to haue praise.
Iigges and ditties of fond loues,
Youth to mickle follie mooues.
And tould this old said saw to thee,
Which Coridon did learne to me,
Tis shame and sin for pregnant wits,
To spend their skill in wanton fits.
Martiall was a bonnie boy,
He writ loues griefe and loues ioy.
He tould what wanton lookes passes,
Twixt the Swaines and the lasses.
And mickle wonder did he write,
Of Womens loues and their spight,
But for the follies of his pen,
He was hated of most men:
For they could say, t'was sin and shame
For Schollers to endite such game.
Quaint was Ouid in his rime,
Chiefest Poet of his time.
What he could in wordes rehearse,
Ended in a pleasing verse.
Apollo with his ay-greene baies,
Crownd his head to shew his praise:
And all the Muses did agree,
He should be theirs, and none but he.
This Poet chaunted all of loue,
Of Cupids wings and Venus doue:
Of faire Corima and her hew,
Of white and red, and vaines blew.
How they loued and how they greed,
And how in fancy they did speed.
His Elegies were wanton all,
Telling of loues pleasings thrall,
And cause he would the Poet seeme,
That best of Venus lawes could deeme.
Strange precepts he did impart,
And writ three bookes of loues art.
There he taught how to woe,
What in loue men should doe,
How they might soonest winne,

Honest women vnto sinne:
Thus to tellen all the truth,
He infected Romes youth:
And with his bookes and verses brought
That men in Rome nought els saught,
But how to tangle maid or wife,
With honors breach throgh wanton life:
The foolish sort did for his skill,
Praise the deepnesse of his quill:
And like to him said there was none,
Since died old Anacreon.
But Romes Augustus worlds wonder,
Brookt not of this foolish blonder:
Nor likt he of this wanton verse,
That loues lawes did rehearse.
For well he saw and did espie,
Youth was sore impaird thereby:
And by experience he finds,
Wanton bookes infect the minds,
Which made him straight for reward,
Though the censure seemed hard,
To bannish Ouid quite from Rome,
This was great Augustus doome:
For (quoth he) Poets quils,
Ought not for to teach men ils.
For learning is a thing of prise,
To shew precepts to make men wise.
And neere the Muses sacred places
Dwels the virtuous minded graces.
Tis shame and sinne then for good wits,
To shew their skill in wanton fits
This Augustus did reply,
And as he said, so thinke I.

LXXXV

THE DESCRIPTION OF SIR GEFFERY CHAWCER

His stature was not very tall,
Leane he was, his legs were small,
Hosd within a stock of red,
A buttond bonnet on his head,
From vnder which did hang, I weene,
Siluer haires both bright and sheene,
His beard was white, trimmed round,
His countnance blithe and merry found,

A Sleeuelesse Iacket large and wide,
With many pleights and skirts side,
Of water Chamlet did he weare,
A whittell by his belt he beare,
His shooes were corned broad before,
His Inckhorne at his side he wore,
And in his hand he bore a booke,
Thus did this auntient Poet looke.

LXXXVI

THE DESCRIPTION OF JOHN GOWER

Large he was, his height was long,
Broad of brest, his lims were strong,
But couller pale, and wan his looke,
Such haue they that plyen their booke,
His head was gray and quaintly shorne,
Neately was his beard worne.
His visage graue, sterne and grim,
Cato was most like to him.
His Bonnet was a Hat of blew,
His sleeues straight of that same hew,
A surcoate of a tawnie die,
Hung in pleights ouer his thigh,
A breech close vnto his dock,
Handsomd with a long stock,
Pricked before were his shoone,
He wore such as others doone,
A bag of red by his side,
And by that his napkin tide,
Thus Iohn Gower did appeare,
Quaint attired as you heere.

LXXXVII

THEODORAS SONG

Secret alone, and silent in my bed,
When follies of my youth doe touch my thought,
And reason tels me that all flesh is sinne,
And all is vaine that so by man is wrought.
        Hearts sighes,
        Eies teares,

With sorrow throb when in my mind I see,
All that man doth is foolish vanitie.

When pride presents the state of honors pompe,
And seekes to set aspiring mindes on fire,
When wanton Loue brings beauty for a bait,
To scortch the eie with ouer hot desire.
      Hearts sighes,
      Eies teares,
With sorrow throb when in my mind I see,
That pride and loue are extreame vanitie.

Oh Loue that ere I loued, yet loue is chast,
My fancie likt none but my husbands face.
But when I thinke I loued none but him,
Nor would my thought giue any other grace,
      Harts sighes,
      Eyes teares,
With sorrow throb, when in my minde I see,
The purest loue is toucht with Iealousie.

Alas mine eye had neuer wanton lookes,
A modest blush did euer taint my Cheekes,
If then suspition with a faulse conceipt.
The ruine of my fame and honour seekes,
      Harts sighes,
      Eyes teares,
Must needs throb sorrows, when my mind doth see,
Chaste thoughts are blamd with causelesse iealousie.

My husbands will was ere to me a lawe.
To please his fancie is my whole delight.
Then if he thinkes whatsoeuer I do is bad,
And with suspition chastitie requight,
      Harts sighes,
      Eyes teares,
Must needs throb sorrows, when my minde dooth see,
Dutie and loue are quit with iealousie.

No deeper hell can fret a womans minde,
Then to be tainted with a false suspect.
Then if my constant thoughts be ouercrost,
When pratling fond, can yeeld no true detect,
      Harts sighes,
      Eyes teares,
Must needs throb sorrows, when my minde doth see,
Duty and loue are quit with iealousie.

Seeke I to please, he thinkes I flatter then,
Obedience is a couer for my fault,
When thus he deemes I treade my shoo awrie.
And going right, he still suspects I halt,
> Harts sighes,
> Eyes teares,
Must needs throb sorrows, when my minde doth see,
Dutie and loue are quit with iealousie.

No salue I haue to cure this restlesse soare,
But sighes to God, to change his iealious minde,
Then shall I praise him in applauding himns,
And when the want of this mistrust I finde,
> Harts sighes,
> Eyes teares,
Shall cease, and Lord ile onely pray to thee,
That women neare be wrongd with iealousie,

LXXXVIII

THE DESCRIPTION OF SALOMON

His stature tall, large, and hie,
Lim'd and featur'd beauteouslie,
Chest was broad armes were strong.
Lockes of Amber passing long,
That hung and waued vpon his necke,
Heauens beautie might they checke.
Visage faire and full of grace,
Mild and sterne, for in one place,
Sate mercie meeklie in his eie:
And Iustice in his lookes hard by.
His Roabes of Bisse, were crimsen hew,
Bordred round with twines of blew:
In Tyre no richer silke solde,
Ouer braided all with golde:
Costly set with pretious stone,
Such before I neere saw none.
A massie Crowne vpon his head,
Checquerd through with Rubies red.
Orient Pearle and bright Topace,
Did burnish out each valiant place.
Thus this Prince that seemed sage,
Did goe in royall Equipage.

Robert Greene - A Short Biography

Robert Greene was, by the best accounts available, born in Norwich in 1558 and baptised on July 11th.

As can be understood much of his early life was not recorded and few contemporary accounts exist to add to what we know. Greene is believed to have attended Norwich Grammar School but did attend Cambridge and received his in 1580, and an M.A. in 1583. He took no part, that we know of, in any of the Cambridge university dramatic productions. Academically he seemed to be nothing above fair. For his B.A. he graduated 38th out of the 41 students in his college, and 115th out of the total graduating class of 1580 of 205 students. For his M.A. it is believed, but not entirely proven, that he transferred to Clare College and was placed 5th out of the 12 students there, and 29th of the 129 students at the university graduating in that year.
But life was about to change. He moved to London and began an extraordinary chapter in his life and career as a widely published author. He was prolific, and of quality, publishing across many genres such as romances, plays and autobiography.
Greene's literary career began with the publication of the long romance, Mamillia, which was entered in the Stationers' Register on 3rd October 1580. Greene's romances were written in a highly wrought style which reached its peak in Pandosto (1588) and Menaphon (1589). Short poems and songs that he incorporated in some of the romances attest to his ability as a lyric poet. One song from Menaphon, 'Weep not my wanton, smile upon my knee, (a mother's lullaby to her baby son)', enjoyed immense success.

Within the space of a few years Greene had published over twenty-five works in prose across several genres and is regarded as 'England's first celebrity author'.

In 1588, he was granted an MA from Oxford University, almost certainly as a courtesy degree. Thereafter he sometimes placed the phrase 'Utruisq. Academiae in Artibus Magister', 'Master of Arts in both Universities' on the title page of his works.

As previously mentioned enough facts on Greene's life are not available so much is made of his autobiographical work 'The Repentance of Robert Greene', In it, Greene claimed to have travelled to Italy and Spain; however, no evidence of Greene's continental trip has been found. Indeed, some scholars doubt that 'The Repentance of Robert Greene' was actually written by the man himself.

In another section of the book Greene claimed to have married a gentleman's daughter, whom he abandoned after having had a child by her and spent her dowry, after which she went to Lincolnshire, and he to London. In 'Four Letters and Certain Sonnets' (1592), Gabriel Harvey prints a letter allegedly written by Greene to his wife in which he addresses her as 'Doll'. However, research through the ages has failed to find any further evidence or record of this marriage. Perhaps it really is indeed a complete fiction and not even by him.

According to 'The Repentance of Robert Greene', Greene is alleged to have written 'A Groatsworth of Wit Bought with a Million of Repentance' during the month leading up to his death, including in it a letter to his wife asking her to forgive him and writing that he was sending their son back to her.

No record of facts survives to validate this. Again in 'Four Letters and Certain Sonnets', Gabriel Harvey claimed that Greene kept a mistress, Em, the sister of a criminal known as 'Cutting Ball' and later hanged at Tyburn. She is described as 'a sorry ragged quean of whom Greene had his base son Infortunatus Greene'.

The facts may be hidden but thankfully much of his work survives. He was perhaps one of the first English authors to support himself with his pen in an age when professional authorship was virtually unknown.

In his 'coney-catching' pamphlets, Greene portrays himself as a well-known public figure, narrating colourful inside stories of rakes and rascals duping young gentlemen and solid citizens out of their hard-earned money. These stories, told from the perspective of a repentant former rascal, have been considered autobiographical, and have been thought to incorporate many facts of Greene's own life thinly veiled as fiction: his early riotous living, his marriage and desertion of his wife and child for the sister of a notorious character of the London underworld, his dealings with players, and his success in the production of plays for them. However, the alternate account suggests that Greene invented almost everything, part of his undoubted skills of being a writer.

In addition to his prose works, Greene also wrote several plays, none of them published in his lifetime, including 'The Scottish History of James IV', 'Alphonsus', and his greatest popular success, 'Friar Bacon and Friar Bungay', as well as 'Orlando Furioso', based on Ludovico Ariosto's Orlando Furioso.

His plays earned himself the title as one of the 'University Wits', including George Peele, Thomas Nashe, and Christopher Marlowe.

As was common with the better talents of the time many works were latter attributed to their hand by unscrupulous printers and publishers eager to put a better name on the title page in their pursuit of sales. Greene has been proposed as the author of several dramas, including a second part to 'Friar Bacon' which may survive as 'John of Bordeaux', 'The Troublesome Reign of King John', 'George a Greene', 'Fair Em', 'A Knack to Know a Knave', 'Locrine', 'Selimus', and 'Edward III', and even Shakespeare's 'Titus Andronicus' and 'Henry VI' plays.

Greene is most familiar to Shakespeare scholars for his pamphlet Greene's 'Groats-Worth of Wit', which alludes to a line, "O tiger's heart wrapped in a woman's hide", found in Shakespeare's Henry VI, Part 3 (c. 1591–92):

'... for there is an upstart Crow, beautified with our feathers, that with his Tygers hart wrapt in a Players hyde, supposes he is as well able to bombast out a blanke verse as the best of you: and being an absolute Johannes fac totum, is in his owne conceit the onely Shake-scene in a countrey.'

Greene's complaint of an actor who states he can write as well as university-educated playwrights, alludes to the actor with a quote that appears in both the True Tragedy quarto and Shakespeare's Folio version of Henry VI, Part 3, and uses the term 'Shake-scene', a unique term never used before or after Greene's screed, to refer to the actor.

Robert Greene died 3rd September 1592, at the very young age of 34.

His death and burial were announced by Gabriel Harvey in a letter to Christopher Bird of Saffron Walden dated 5th September, first published as a 'butterfly pamphlet' about 8th September, and later expanded as 'Four Letters and Certain Sonnets', entered in the Stationers' Register on 4th December 1592.

However, no record of Greene's burial has ever been found.

Robert Greene – A Concise Bibliography

Prose works
Mamillia: A Mirror or Looking-glass for the Ladies of England (1583)
Mamillia: The Second Part of the Triumph of Pallas (1593)
The Anatomy of Lovers' Flatteries (1584)
The Myrrour of Modestie (1584)
Arbasto; The Anatomy of Fortune (1584)
Gwydonius; The Card of Fancy (1584)
The Debate Between Folly and Love (1584)
The Second Part of the Tritameron of Love (1587)
Planetomachia (1585)
An Oration or Funeral Sermon (1585)
Morando; The Tritameron of Love (1587)
Morando; The Second Part of the Tritameron of Love (1587)
Euphues: His Censure to Philautus (1587)
Greene's Farewell to Folly (1591)
Penelope's Web (c1587)
Alcida; Greene's Metamorphosis (1617)
Greenes Orpharion (1599)
Pandosto (1588)
Perimedes (1588)
Ciceronis Amor (1589)
Menaphon (1589)
The Spanish Masquerado (1589)
Greene's Mourning Garment (1590)
Greene's Never Too Late (1590)
Francesco's Fortunes, or The Second Part of Greene's Never Too Late (1590)
Greene's Vision, Written at the Instant of his Death (c1590)
The Royal Exchange (1590)
A Notable Discovery of Coosnage (1591)
The Second Part of Conycatching (1591)
The Black Books Messenger (1592)
A Disputation Between a Hee Conny-Catcher and a Shee Conny-Catcher (1592)
A Groatsworth of Wit Bought with a Million of Repentance (1592)
Philomela (1592)
A Quip for an Upstart Courtier (1592)
The Third and Last Part of Conycatching (1592)

Verse
A Maiden's Dream (1591)

Plays
Friar Bacon and Friar Bungay (circa 1590)
The History of Orlando Furioso (circa 1590)
A Looking Glass for London and England (with Thomas Lodge) (circa 1590)
The Scottish History of James the Fourth (circa 1590)
The Comical History of Alphonsus, King of Aragon (circa 1590)
Selimus (circa 1594)

www.ingramcontent.com/pod-product-compliance
Lightning Source LLC
Chambersburg PA
CBHW021936040426
42448CB00008B/1101